DEAD IN A DITCH

Growing Up In Texas & Other Near-Death Experiences

This is a memoir, of sorts; essays to chew on and ponder

BY JODY SEAY

Koho Pono, LLC

Dead in a Ditch

Published by Koho Pono, LLC
Clackamas, Oregon USA
http://KohoPono.com

For general information on our other products, please contact our Customer Service
Department within the USA at 503-723-7392 or visit http://KohoPono.com

First Edition 8september2011

Library of Congress Control Number: 2011933618

ISBN: 978-0-9845424-4-4

Manufactured in the United States of America

"If you have ever known - or been - a mother who feared everything bad would happen to your children - lockjaw, snake bites, the atomic bomb, communism, and finding them 'dead in a ditch', then you must read Jody Seay's hilarious account of her own mother's anxieties.

Read it even if you fear that reading makes you go blind. Here is an Earth Daughter raised by an Earth Mother. The result is a Texas-size funny book about both."

> - Liz Carpenter, author of Getting Better All The Time, Ruffles And Flourishes, Unplanned Parenthood, and Start With A Laugh and former press secretary for Lady Bird Johnson

"Jody Seay handed me this book and said, 'I hope you laugh so hard you bust your spleen.' I'm happy to say that my spleen survived intact - but my pancreas is still in a splint. Jody Seay is ONE FUNNY WRITER."

> - Jerry Juhl, three-time Emmy Award winner, former head writer for The Muppets and Jim Henson Productions, screenwriter for The Muppet Movie and Muppets Treasure Island, head writer for The Muppet Show

Dead In A Ditch is the hilarious memoir of a tomboy Texan, a little (and then not-so-little) comic hellion who takes every dare. Jody Seay is also a worry-wart. How many ways in Texas can you die if you're not careful? If the snakes don't getcha the atom bomb will, and in the meantime, watch out for lockjaw! A smart, funny tough survivor of a goofy family and her own weird antics, Seay (pronounced See) is one helluva writer and a great observer of the absurdities and poignancy of family life in Texas."

> - Robin Cody, Author of Another Way the River Has, Ricochet River and Voyage of a Summer Sun; Pacific Northwest Bookseller Association Book Award Winner and Oregon Book Award Winner

"You can feel, hear, taste and smell your own childhood - with a Texas accent - in Jody Seay's stories. When you stop laughing, you find here and there a shaping truth about your own life that's eluded expression all these years. You want to read this book."

-Jeff Golden, author of Forest Blood, and public radio personality

"Jody Seay is a story-teller extraordinaire. Her wonderfully funny and insightful work has universal appeal. With her page-turning writing, she has that rare gift of being able to touch the hearts and minds of a broad and varied audience."

-Nina McIntosh, MSW, author of The Educated Heart: Professional Guidelines For Massage Therapists, Bodyworkers And Movement Teachers

"There are writers and there are WRITERS. But every now and then a monster writing talent rockets into the literary world from seemingly out of nowhere. Such a writer is Jody Seay. I have known Jody for years, and have never ceased to be simply amazed by every piece of work that flows from this women's pen. Lively, insightful, heartbreaking, and laugh-til-you-barf funny...yes, of course, but Jody brings even more to the table. There is a depth to her work that simply defies description. Jody's stories are to be tasted, then munched, then gobbled up whole and juicy like warm pie. Writing just doesn't get any better than this. Sit down with her book, and get ready for a feast."

- Susan Chernak McElroy, best-selling author of Animals As Teachers And Healers, and Animals As Guides For The Soul

Dedication

This book is dedicated to my family - all of them Texan to the bone.

*"Now, you boys know better than to try and
sneak past your Mother. Your Mother could hear
a rat piss on cotton." - 1969, Warren Seay to his
teenage sons, Pat and Mike*

In loving memory of my brother Dean, the hero, and of my brother Pat, the good guy.

For Stef, as is everything I do.

Acknowledgements

Most writers have many cheerleaders. I am no exception. We need them.

My apologies to so many who kept asking about my next book after The Second Coming of Curly Red was published. I am sorry this has taken me so long; it seems my horse went lame on me there for a while. Now, it feels good to be back in the saddle. My thanks to all of you who have never given up on me even when I did, especially those of you who are now partying over this up in Heaven: Shirley Hudgens, Janie French, Randy Toups, Nina McIntosh, Lou Kimberling, Gay Lustfield, Geneice Gray and CarolAnn Kerman. I miss all of you every day.

On this level, my gratitude goes to those of you who knew I'd finally get off my tail and get it all down in a book some day: Stef Neyhart, Sue Sullivan, Margaret Quinn, Jan Treybig, Sheryl Reese, Sharla Taylor, Nicholas French, Ira Lipson, Melinda Pittman, Stephen Saunders, Judith & Tina, Laura Caraway, Cynthia Griffin, Mike Lindberg, Don Gleason, "Q" & Mary, Millie & Diana, Cheryl & Melody, Jan & Joyce, Rikki LeBaron, Gayl & Osima, Marnie & Joey, Sheri & Linda, McKenzie Kerman, Lisa Yeo & the GNO group, Beth Sawyer, Judy Wood, Lynne Webb, Polk Green, Lynda Jacobs, Catherine Reed, Robin Kendall, OSU Media Services and the Back Page crew, the Porter/McCormick family, the Cobble family, the Dorwart family, the Duke family, and the people I love who lived the stories here, my family.

Big hugs and thanks to all my Rolfing clients who've been trapped in their underpants listening to these stories over and over all these years. If I've left anyone out, I beg forgiveness. I am beyond grateful to all of you for your love, your support, your encouragement, your confidence and your friendship. It makes my world shine.

Jody Seay

Table of Contents

Introduction

I was born with a birthmark and an attitude, only one of which could ever be removed. The lumpy, strawberry malformation on my right forearm was burned away with dry ice in some pediatrician's office leaving a dip and a jagged scar in the skin with which I used to cheat when it was time to tell my right from my left as a child. I knew my scar was on my right arm; the other one, well, what was left was my left, right? As I got older, I made up different stories about it - a knife fight, gunshot, rattlesnake bite - dangerous stories designed to make me appear brave. No smart person ever believed me.

My attitude was a whole different deal. It was as permanent as a cattle brand, glommed onto my DNA like a saddle blanket and as soaked through me as the place of my birth, Texas, where women who aren't born a smarty-pants, as I was, will learn soon enough how to take that one on.

Heaven's way of insuring that I would see the humor in most of life's situations was to launch me into the world under unusual circumstances. My mother's water broke with me at the Spike Jones concert at Fair Park in Dallas on Oct. 25, 1949. I was born dry and breech two days later - tiny, two months early, and with my chest caved in - an impatient, silent and brooding baby - not even sure I wanted to stick around. I was the unanticipated by-product of my divorcing parents having wished each other "luck" at the Hotel Dallas just before their final farewell. On the fifth day of my life, a nurse came into my mother's hospital room and said, "Well, she finally cried today." And I've not hushed since. Ask anybody.

Mother remarried and our stepfather, the man we called "Daddy," adopted my older brother and me. Then Mother gave birth to twin boys and, a few years later, to our baby sister, which completed her dream of being able to sign our Christmas cards "The Seven

Seays." It was a simple thing which brought her much joy, God knows why.

Daddy's family owned a cattle ranch up by Nocona, Texas - yes, where they make those boots - and Mother's family was from Forestburg, Texas, a small ranching and farming town, so we grew up riding horses and playing cowboy, even though we were city kids from Dallas. Round-ups and rodeos were more real than fantasy in our childhood, something we've always been grateful for, and all of us know our way around a horse. Nobody in my family, however, ever looked anything like J.R., Sue Ellen or any of the Dallas crowd that showed up on television years later. Shoot, Dallas didn't even look like Dallas.

In my childhood, Dallas was a city remaking itself over and over again. Begun as a trading post next to a dirty, shallow river, and expanding in all directions each year, it kept defying the odds to survive. It was a city with no real reason for being there. Now it is a massive metropolis full of people willing to put up with the heat of a Texas summer (which I wasn't) to be able to call themselves Texans (which I still do.)

I come from a large family. My Mother's biggest fear was that one or all of us would die on her watch when we were babies and then children. As we grew up, her fear shifted a little - not just that we would die, but that we would be found Dead in a Ditch. It was the ditch part that always made it seem so much worse, something drug or alcohol related, to be sure. Mother's children crumpled up and tossed out the window like an old beer can. "Where have you been?" she would say, "I was worried sick. I thought you were dead in a ditch." This was her mantra.

I am the family historian for our branch of the family tree, primarily because I have a good memory, so when cousins and siblings need to know some obscure tidbit of family info, I'm usually the one who gets the call. I also know that a memoir means that it is being written from memory and, often, everybody's memory of an event can be different. While I thought the family reunion was just swell, I realize somebody else might have been pouting in the car with their feelings hurt. I have tried my best here to tell the stories as I remember them without swiping anybody else's thunder, anybody else's story, or embellishing them too much beyond what they were. It is all as true as I can get it without an injection of sodium pentothal. So, there you have it.

Mother has been gone for two decades now; my older brother since 2005. My baby brother Pat, one of the world's truly good guys, left us in 2007, surrounded by so much love from family and friends it made my heart crack in two. For those of us still around, as we trundle off toward the second half our time here, my hope is that our lives and our deaths will be easy and sweet - and ditchless.

- Jody Seay

"I am two with nature." - Woody Allen

Chapter 1 – Snakes

We spent an extraordinary amount of our childhood appearing to be flash-frozen. This was due to snakes.

Big snakes, little snakes, snakes with teeth, snakes without teeth, snakes with venom and without, snakes that would squeeze and strangle the life out of you, snakes that wouldn't bother with you, snakes that couldn't even hold on, snakes that ran away at the sight of humans. It didn't matter. In the eyes of Mother, a snake was a snake was a snake, and even if the snake you managed to encounter had slithered away, terrified, long before you even had a chance to freeze, frozen is how you should stay. She never told us for how long, and I once stayed frozen like a mannequin in the woods behind our house, almost certain I'd seen a snake, until Daddy came looking for me to come in for supper.

"What the hell are you doing?" he said.

"Shhhhh," I whispered out of the corner of my mouth. "Snake."

"Where?"

"Don't know." My mouth was moving like a hand puppet. Sweat streamed down my little mask of a face.

"How long have you been standing here like this?"

"Since Dean got back from school. He got tired and walked home. Did he get bit?"

"No, and that snake has probably died of old age by now. Come on to the house."

Snakes

If we had spent all our time in Dallas, snakes would probably not have been something my Mother was constantly sure would kill us, but Daddy's family had a ranch near Nocona, Texas and Mother's family was from a tiny country town called Forestburg, so we spent quite a bit of time playing cowboy in both places.

Dressed in our western duds, anxious to saddle up and get riding, we couldn't leave the house without Mother's typical lecture on what we should do if we encountered a snake of any sort. Any color. Any length. Any distance. Anywhere. No exceptions.

"If you're walking out to the corral and you see a snake..."

"If you reach in the barn to get a bucket of oats and you see a snake..."

"If you grab for the hose and there's a snake..."

"If you go into the tack room and you see a snake..."

"If you're riding close to rocks and you see a snake..."

"If you stop to water the horses and you see a snake..."

"If you're riding under some thick trees and you look up and see a snake..."

"If you get thrown off your horse and land on a snake..."

"If you have to get off to take the horses through a gate and you see a snake..."

"If you bring the horses back into the corral and you see a snake..."

"If you take off the bridle and turn around and there's a snake..."

And on and on and on and on... snakes could be anywhere and everywhere, all at once. In Mother's eyes, there was no safe place. "Oh," she'd say, "when you go to bed, pull the covers all the way back and check for snakes before you climb in."

At Aunt Roxie's house, I thought, *was she kidding? A snake wouldn't be able to breathe in there.*

Aunt Roxie pulled her sheets so tight it made my feet bend out to either side in a perfect V. I was always lucky the next day to get my cowboy boots to track straight ahead. If I gritted my teeth and tried to keep my toes straight up, I'd wake up with my feet looking like a pixie's until I'd had time to stomp around and bring my toes back to normal. *A snake in one of Aunt Roxie's beds? I don't think so. Not unless the snake was on a suicide mission.*

But I checked anyway. "You just never know," Mother always said. Nobody understood the full potential of impending doom like my Mother. Of this, I was certain.

Earlier in our lives, when we lived out in the country for a year in Palestine, Texas, my brother and I had a log cabin playhouse near the woods. Daddy ran over an albino rattlesnake with the lawnmower one day not far from our playhouse and from that day forth Dean and I were forced to wear boots - Mother's, not our own - whenever we ventured out there. Dean wore Mother's tall English riding boots and I wore her cowboy boots. Seeing as how we were only four and five years old at the time, we fell over a lot as we clomped around through the grass and leaves in boots that were way, way too big for us.

Rattlesnakes and copperheads had a perfect shot at our tiny faces as we fwammed! to the ground. When Mother's riding boots began rubbing Dean's groin raw, we were pardoned and got to wear our own boots again, sometimes even our tennis shoes. I guess Daddy convinced Mother that snakebite was much less of a chance (and probably less painful) than a scraped and bloody little pair of nuts.

Snakes

After Dean started school, I kept up my morbid fascination with snakes and devised my own method of protection to keep them at bay - voodoo, straight from the brain of a five year old. The school bus would roar and rattle away with my brother on it each morning and I would stand at the corner of the gravel road and wave to him. As soon as I could take a deep breath again over the dust, I would look around at my feet until I found the three most perfect stones. Setting them in a line, either one way or the other from the corner, I would whisper, three times, "Snakes can't come across this," as if snakes came barreling in droves right down our road each morning, suddenly losing control, skidding off onto our grass, and waiting right there all morning for me to glide past on my tricycle where they could grab hold of my ankle with their venom-dripping teeth and not let go until I was filled with poison and all the blood had been drained from my body.

Of course, the wondrous part (to me, at least) was that I never got nailed by a snake, which only proved that my voodoo technique was working. However, the more rocks I piled up, the more the edge of our yard began to resemble a slapped-together shrine and Daddy made me stop doing it. Then, certain that snakebite was only moments away, I began kneeling by the rose bushes and praying for Divine Guidance and protection to our TV antenna, which bore a striking resemblance to the cross above the pulpit at church. This tactic seemed to work pretty well, also; at least, nobody got bitten on my watch.

I became obsessed with snakes. I wore the cover off the September, 1953 National Geographic magazine's issue about snakes. With both fascination and fear I looked at it like a canary stares at the python about to swallow it whole. I could not yet read, but it didn't matter. The pictures were more than enough to terrify me over and over, tightening my bowels and stiffening my neck, especially the picture of the diamondback rattlesnake, fierce-looking, poised and ready to strike right at my throat.

Sitting on the couch, the magazine on my lap, my legs only long enough to stick straight out, I would turn the pages slowly, ... slowly, ... slower ... until I got to the page just before the rattler. My heart would pound, the timpani sound of it bonging in my head like paint buckets full of my own blood banging around in a steel drum. A thin veil of sweat would glisten on my forehead and beads of it would form under my eyes and across the bridge of my nose. My breath would come in shallow, ragged bursts. My mouth would be pulled tight into a thin little line, and peeking out, like a tiny pink triangle, would be the tip of my tongue.

Without warning, I would strike! I flipped the page, taking that diamond back by surprise, and I held the magazine up to my face so that the snake and I were eyeball to beady eyeball, staring each other down, our rattlers poised and buzzing. I was ready for this showdown, yessir. *One...two...three...four...five*, I would count in my head, as if five was the magic number, the exact amount of seconds I instinctively knew it would take for the rattler to see the determination in my squinty little brown eyes. He would slink away then, coward that he was. After five seconds he would know he was no match for me as I fought to protect my family from snakes. This was my mission.

Everything I saw, everything that moved (or didn't) then became a snake, vicious and mean and full of poison, ready to fling itself straight at me, ready to sink its fangs deep into my skin and leave me a writhing, gasping purple mess on the edge of the road.

When I wasn't busy "freezing" at the sight of snakes, imagined or otherwise, I was fighting back. I chopped a croquet mallet left behind in the grass almost to pieces with a hoe, so certain was I that it was a rattler cleverly disguising himself as a piece of harmless family game equipment and waiting for the chance to snuff some unsuspecting member of my clan.

On the outside, I appeared to be a regular happy-go-lucky, playful, almost carefree child. Inwardly, though, I was a knotted ball of angst with my entire central nervous system on red alert, ready for fight or flight. Or freeze, of course, which had become my specialty.

My eyes darted around like a criminal's whenever we were outside. I scanned the yard, the garage, the road and the driveway for danger - every inch of it. Mother couldn't even load the twins into the car until I'd checked under the seat for snakes. Only after I'd inspected it, could anyone reach into the mailbox. Or the dog house. Or the diaper bag. Or the toy box. Or anyplace a viper might be lying in wait.

I took to carrying a flashlight constantly and wearing a butter knife through the belt loop on my pants. Mother wouldn't let me have anything sharper, even when I told her I was sure she'd be sorry about this. No way would she order a rifle for me out of the Sears & Roebuck Catalog. "You can just forget that big idea," is what she said.

I begged her for a snakebite kit. When she refused, I devised my own from some old rubber Spoolies, bobbie pins, tweezers, safety pins, and adhesive tape. I stuffed all of these into a sock, rolled it up and carried it in my pocket at all times. When I slept, my snakebite kit stayed under my pillow. Mother washed it twice by mistake when she changed the sheets.

"Just what," she asked the first time, "is this?"

"Snakebite kit," I said.

"Are you expecting a snakebite?" she asked.

"You never know," I said, mimicking what I'd heard from her from the time I was old enough to pay attention and understand.

"That's true," she said, realizing this monster she'd created with her own fears was also her daughter. "You just never know," she muttered.

Some people are fascinated by snakes and love, love, love them. That's not me. I am fascinated by them and still want nothing to do with them. I don't want to hold them, or kiss on them, or even have them hug my neck. You just never know when one might get carried away and forget that this is hugging and not dinner which needs to be squeezed into an edible form.

And I don't want to wake one up and piss it off, either. Several lifetimes ago, when I was still trying to fool myself into believing I was heterosexual, a young man I was seeing saw me for the very last time over one simple remark. We were smooching in a rather vigorous fashion. "Uh-oh," he said, "the snake is awake."

"Snake?" I asked, "Awake?" My ears began to pound at the mention of the word.

He pointed to his pants. *His weenis? A snake? Oh, dear God, how could that obvious similarity have escaped me?* All my passion for him zoomed right out the window like smoke through a Vent-A-Hood. I shot up from the couch as if I were spring-loaded, grabbed my coat and headed for the door faster than you could say coitus interruptus, if that is something you would ever say, although probably not.

As I ran I spewed words in one big gush. "I forgot," I said, "I'm already involved with someone, practically engaged, really, he's burly and mean and jealous, and he wouldn't like this one bit, nope, not a bit, he has tattoos and a big mustache, and he's really good with guns, whew - how could I ever forget that! Ha ha ha! We met at a shooting range, we were both doing target practice, and wow, is he ever good at it, yes he is, sometimes I wonder if he's ever killed anybody, he gets so mad - boy, wouldn't that be something - Ha ha ha! Plus, I have to get to the dry cleaner's before they close, and,...uh,...oh yeah, I think I left a pot of beans boiling on the stove, so, `bye'." Panicked, I gave every good excuse I could think of at once.

My friend Sylvia, the science teacher, bought her son a boa constrictor for his birthday. They named him Clutch, as I recall, and he lived in an empty fish tank on a branch with a light bulb over it to keep him warm. He did mostly nothing except look bored and creepy and mean. I hated him. Sylvia's family thought he was darling, though, just the cutest thing they'd ever seen, which proves what we've always thought about the strangeness of science teachers, and also that there's just no accounting for taste.

Each day Sylvia slid on her butt down a hill behind their house and captured field mice to feed the snake. (For the life of me, I could never figure out just how she did this; she was a better mouser than any cat I'd ever seen). "Come on in here," she said when I stopped by, "Clutch is about to eat dinner," and she proceeded to dangle a mouse close enough to the snake's mouth for him to grab, which he did. I watched this horror through my fingers. Clutch tried to gulp, but couldn't. His jaws cranked back open, and then the most amazing thing happened - the rodent backed right straight out of the snake's mouth!

Slamming his little body into high-gear reverse, the mouse had stared into the abyss and said, "Nuh-uh." Clutch tried again, and once more, the mouse made it all the way back out of the snake's throat - what a guy!

Back out, buddy, back out, buddy, back out, buddy, I said in my head, cheering for this tiny creature who had apparently envisioned an entirely different version of his own demise, one that did not involve a snake. Even survival-of-the-fittest, eco-system-loving Sylvia had to admit that this mouse deserved his freedom after such a fight. We named him "Reprieve" and thought about painting the tip of one his paws with fingernail polish, possibly a bright tangerine shade called "Escape" or an angry zit-looking reddish tone, maybe, something called "Breakout" so that, just in case she ever caught him again she would know to let him go. The mark would be his own tiny red badge of courage.

Such chutzpah and startling determination should never go without its own reward, and that's a good thing. I was so proud of the mouse, but I must say it still didn't make me like the snake any better. I don't think anything ever could.

Of course, that which we resist persists, and snakes have found their way to me over the years, possibly to offer an olive branch of peace if only I'd stuck around long enough to get to know them and not run off screaming, with my hair standing on end.

At Lake Texoma when I was in my early twenties, I sat on a dock and dangled my feet in the water, just enjoying the day, waiting on my brother Mike so we could go for a boat ride. I don't know how long the little copperhead who'd wrapped himself around my ankle had been there, resting, just enjoying the day, like me, before I saw him. Having spent a good part of the summer outdoors, I had a pretty good tan, but suddenly all the color drained from everywhere on my body. My legs now looked like two pieces of raw chicken dangling in the lake.

I froze, of course, realizing I had become lunch. *What am I going to do,* I wondered. *I am screwed, I know it.*

Mike walked up. "Ready to go, Sis?" he asked.

I couldn't move, couldn't even speak, so terrified was I of spooking the copperhead. I had to do something, say something, but I didn't want to make anything close to a hissing sound. I didn't want the snake to somehow think I was his competition.

"'nnnnnnnnake," I whispered, forcing the word out just above a whisper. I tried pointing, just slightly, with my index finger. My body began to vibrate and sweat. I'm sure I looked like one of those Rain Bird lawn sprinklers with beads of terror-infused perspiration flying off of me in every direction.

"What?" Mike said, "Are you all right?"

"`nnnnnnnnake," I repeated, sweat running down beside my ears.

"You sound like you've had a stroke," Mike said. He walked over just as the little snake unraveled himself and swam away. "Oh, shit!" Mike yelled, jumping back, 'that was a copperhead. I didn't know they could swim!"

"And I didn't know," I said, pulling my feet out of the water and up under me as I sank back onto the dock with a beach towel slung over my face, "that they could use me as a bus stop."

Even now, so very many, many, years later, when Big Jim Fowler or some reptile-smooching snake-lover appears on one of the television morning talk shows, I start to cringe. Sure enough, just as I knew would happen, some guy in a khaki shirt wants to drape a bored, creepy and mean-looking boa constrictor around the shoulders of lovely and smooth Meredith Viera or lay a twenty-eight foot python across some beautiful and cool morning show hostess's arms. It is then that the voice in my head starts screaming, "*Don't do it, Meredith! It's a snake, man; those sneaky bastards will get you!*" or "*Stop! Drop that thing and run!*"

Of course, as I've aged, and since I don't live in the country anymore, or even in Texas, I am far less vigilant than I was when I patrolled the yard with my flashlight, butter knife, and snakebite kit at the ready. But I can't say I've become complacent, or that I ever will. Before I stick my hand into the mailbox, that voice always fires off in my head and I stop. I stand on my tippy-toes and peer down into the bottom, just to check. Just to be sure. Yes, it's good to be safe, because, as my Mother always said, "You just never know."

"Here is the test to find out whether your mission
on Earth is finished. If you're alive, it isn't."
- Richard Bach

Chapter 2 – Bad Guys

For most of my childhood, from age three to almost fourteen, perhaps there was no greater terror for my mother than the fear we would be snatched away and harmed by Bad Guys.

But it would have taken one heck of a determined Bad Guy to pull it off. First of all, there were just so many of us kids, any normal Bad Guy would have said, "Forget it, snatching this crew would be too much work." Unless he happened to have a van with blacked-out windows or a station wagon or bus to cart us all away at the same time, we were safe by the sheer number of us, if nothing else.

Secondly, Mother taught us to fight like tigers for the safety of our younger siblings. In preparation for this fine responsibility, my brother Dean and I never passed a hill of any sort without scrambling to the top of it and having a Roy Rogers-type cowboy duke-out and roll all the way to the bottom. We wanted to be ready to use our finely-honed, cowboy-fighting skills to defeat Bad Guys where ever they lurked.

We had other skills, too. My brother could punch a "frog" on anybody's arm, paralyzing them for hours. As for me, I spent many evenings watching 'Saturday Night Wrestling From The Sportatorium' with our grandfather, Daddy Bob, so I could drop any scoundrel with an upside-down-step-over-toe-hold just as reliably as Pepper Gomez, Nick Kovak, or Fritz Von Erich. These were Daddy Bob's favorite wrestlers and my TV mentors. By talent and sheer force of will, I knew I could hold any Bad Guy right where they fell, twisted and pinned until the cops came. And, most likely, I would either kill him or make him repent, which, according to what I just learned in Sunday school, was a good thing.

Lots of the Daddies in my neighborhood, including my own, got drunk on Saturday night and repented on Sunday morning only to do the very same thing the next week. So, to my way of thinking, repenting was not a very effective technique in the long run. To stop the Bad Guy, I'd probably have to go ahead and kill the scalawag.

We had another weapon in our family arsenal to defeat Bad Guys. My younger brothers, the twins Pat and Mike, would have driven any normal person absolutely nuts. They were hardly ever more than two feet away from each other for their entire childhood, except when Mike decided to "hide," which I will explain later. They looked exactly alike, had their own special little twin-speak lingo, and called each other "Dah" until they were almost four. They jabbered constantly, only nobody could understand them except the other twin. Yep, the Bad Guy would have dropped them off at the corner and sped away after an hour of the twin's company.

Truthfully, the only one of the whole pack to worry about was our baby sister, Peggy who would toddle up to total strangers in her high-top baby shoes and stretch her little arms for them to pick her up. If anybody refused, which was rare, she would fall to the floor and sob, resting her little blonde head on her hands, tears streaming down her cheeks and forming a puddle beneath her, her spirit staggering under the burden and shame. *Oh, the pain and the torture of it all!* It was as if her heart had been pierced and the wound would be with her for the rest of her days, a stain on her soul as deep and lasting as grape juice on a baby bib. None of us handled rejection well, but Peggy was the absolute, hands-down, A-1 champ at not handling it well; that was plain right from the get-go. She was a sweet and amazingly trusting child, and yet, she, too, had a secret weapon. Her dimpled smile would have melted the heart of any Bad Guy. He would have changed his wicked ways on the spot. The other four of us adored her and weren't taking any chances so we guarded her like our treasure.

Peggy had a felony-intense Jones for broccoli and chuckled out loud when we made faces at her or squeezed Jell-O through our teeth. My kid sister was also a wonderful toy - a wind-up doll. We could get her to do anything: jump off the washing machine, launch herself from the hutch cabinet, hang from the top of the swing set and drop like a member of the Screaming Eagles straight into somebody's arms.

The problem with our living doll arose when Peggy began doing the tricks on her own with no one around to catch her. She splattered on the floor and screamed her brains out. Not only did she get hurt, she also felt double-crossed. After all, somebody had always caught her before. This is how Mother found out about our secret acrobatics club. We older kids thought the-somebody-there-to-catch-you-part-of-the-equation should have been obvious to Peggy.

"Do you kids want to live in the back yard for the rest of your lives?" Mother hissed as she yanked me by the arm, "She's only two. Do you want to kill your very own sister?"

Well, no, I thought, *of course not. We are sworn to protect her. If we didn't, then we would become the Bad Guys.*

One of our favorite wind-up-doll-tricks was to wait until we parked next to a car packed with important people - police officers, firemen, etc. Dean would roll down the window and I'd hand Peggy over to my brother.

In her best Mae West imitation my innocent baby sister would coo, "Why don't you come up and see me sometime, big boy?"

We kids would laugh hilariously at Mother's reaction. Her neck actually shortened and disappeared into her shoulders, so deep was her cringe. She would slowly drive away, which was an extreme form of restraint for Mother, who generally stomped on that gas pedal so she'd be leader of the pack. She might have been a Mom with a bunch of kids in a Chevy station wagon, but when she got behind the wheel of a car, Jo Seay didn't mess around.

After the cops or firemen had gotten plenty far away from us, I would look in the rearview mirror and see Mother's hazel eyes beginning to turn that blistering shade of green they always became when she was pissed. *Uh-oh.* I would elbow Dean in the ribs so he wouldn't do anything stupid like belching or making fart noises with his armpit and uncork Mother.

"If you kids don't settle down," she would say through teeth clenched tightly enough to crack, "I'm going to sit between you."

Dean and I looked at each other as if Mother had just fallen over the edge - no, as if we had just pushed her there, which is often how I felt whenever we had made her blistering-green-eyed mad. Even so, I could not resist whispering to my brother the words that would get me grounded for a week - no television, no record player, no best friend over to bop with me, and no use of the good crayons until the weekend. "Who will drive the car?" I asked him.

I'm surprised Mother never tracked down some wicked, smelly Bad Guys with tattoos and missing teeth. "Here, just take 'em," I imagined she would say as she handed us over to them. "I've had it. You can't be as bad as they are." Then together Mother and the Bad Guys would throw us into the back of a smashed-up truck and Mother would watch them race off as they slurped rot-gut whiskey and cackled into the night.

But that was never true for her. No matter how bad we were, the Bad Guys were worse - whoever they were, wherever they were, and they were always out there, never a day off, waiting...just waiting...for one of us to let down our guard, which is why Mother always made sure we were in a group. No one knew better than Mother that us as a group was discouraging.

Group safety became especially difficult to maintain the year my brother Mike, one of the twins, learned what a swell thing it was to hide. We should have seen this coming. When he was just a little toddler, he would sit backwards in one of the ladder-backed dining room chairs so that a slat was precisely positioned over his eyes. Like a baby chimp, he thought if he could not see us, then we could not see him. And we supported him perfectly. "Where's Mike?" We'd giggle. "Where is that Michael?" "Where do you think he could have gone?" "Boy, I hope Mike is wearing something warm. It will be so sad around here without our Michael." We played this game over and over, sometimes for hours it seemed.

When Mike had determined that he was sufficiently loved and missed, he would let himself reappear, and we would welcome him back like a lost soldier.

The next year, when I was six, Mike upped the ante. Not only could he hide, he could now run and hide. *Oh boy.* Dean and I sprinted for miles looking for him. Miles. As prone as I am to exaggerations, this is not one of them. I swear this is when my knees first began to give out - searching for my little brother and finding him before the Bad Guys did.

We once snared Mike down at the end of a double block, around the corner, by the park, hiding in the back seat of a teenager's hot rod. He poked his little burr-cut head up just as we ran past and I spotted him out of the corner of my eye.

Mission: successful.

Bad Guys: thwarted.

Another time, he hid in the doghouse all day as Dean and I ran what was the equivalent of a trip from Dallas to Houston searching for him - all day - in the summer - in Texas.

I was constantly on the lookout for Bad Guys, everywhere, every moment. I non-stop worried, *Bad Guys, Snakes and Communists - dear God, how could there be so many terrible things slithering around on the same planet all at once?*

I especially worried about Bad Guys when I helped Aunt Roxie and Uncle Meb run the Post Office in Forestburg, Texas (population

224 or thereabouts). I spent at least a week with them each summer. It was there that I was first introduced to the intricate workings of the U.S. government. I helped Aunt Roxie sell stamps to customers and assisted Uncle Meb in sorting the mail.

Standing on a chair next to the wooden bins, I would hold each piece of mail aloft until Uncle Meb indicated where it should go. He pointed and I chunked, a time-honored postal technique that remains the same to this day. When I was eight, I picked up a package with FRAGILE marked across the bottom. I'd never seen the word before.

"What does it mean?" I asked Uncle Meb.

"It means you throw it left-handed," he replied.

The next summer, when I was nine, I easily recognized the word, threw it left-handed and easily got into the day's routine. After the morning rush was over, Aunt Roxie usually took off for Bowie to go to the chiropractor, or to get her hair done, or to have her glasses checked. I stayed with Uncle Meb who leaned back in his chair, put his feet up on the desk and read other people's magazines for the rest of the day. His was a fairly easy job.

What occupied my time was the big ring of WANTED posters which hung in the lobby. It was a central location so everyone who came into the Post Office could get a good look at these Bad Guys and, hopefully, do their duty by turning them in to the F.B.I.

The first thing I noticed was the tops of these wanted posters were dusty. *Hmmmmm*, I thought, *I may be just a kid, but, according to my deductions, that means these wanted posters are hardly ever looked at. And that,* I continued to muse, *means Forestburg, Texas, is probably crawling with F.B.I. fugitives and crooks of every sort. I'll bet nobody even knows it!*

I mentioned my theory to Aunt Roxie as she roared away in her Buick, but all I could understand of her reply was something about "...all the really big crooks are in Washington..."

At irregular intervals throughout each day, so as not to arouse suspicion, I would climb down off my U.S. Government-issue postal stool, hunker down by the window of the Post Office with the big ring of wanted posters beside me, and examine anyone walking down the street while feverishly flipping through the stack. Or I stood at the edge of the window with my fingers curled around my imaginary artillery field lenses scanning the highway for anyone or anything illegal.

I almost became convinced my Uncle George, who lived right there in Forestburg and walked everywhere because he did not own a car, was wanted for grand theft auto in Arkansas, so closely did he resemble one of the crooks in my stack. I mentioned this to Uncle Meb.

He rolled his eyes. "You don't see him driving a car now, do you?" he asked.

"No."

"Then I doubt he stole one. George hasn't left town since the war."

"Úncle Meb," I asked "do you have any binoculars at home that we could bring to the Post Office so I can keep watch even better?"

"Ah, don't worry about it," Uncle Meb said.

Obviously, Uncle Meb didn't know me all that well. I worried constantly - about almost everything, but especially Bad Guys. *Maybe,* I thought with concern, *if I honed down my list of crooks and concentrate primarily on crime that might involve the use of a weapon, then my vigilance would carry more weight.* Uncle Meb explained crimes to me. Interstate Flight to Avoid Prosecution, for example, didn't seem like such a bad thing. Heck, Robin Hood did that all the time. If I were a crook, I would probably do it, too.

By the end of the second day, I understood the meaning of grand larceny, mail fraud, conspiracy to commit murder, drug possession, armed robbery, grand theft auto, possession of illegal firearms and conspiracy to overthrow the federal government. I already understood murder and rape. When I found a wanted poster on the bottom of the stack I'd never seen before, I knew I'd have to ask Uncle Meb once more, even though I also knew I'd almost pushed him far, far over the edge with my questions from the past two days.

"What's White Slavery?" I asked, out of the blue, and saw the newspaper in front of Uncle Meb's face begin to shake. If I'd had Mother's X-Ray vision and could see clear through Uncle Meb's newspaper and through his body, I probably would have seen his heart suddenly stop, leaving big, muddy scrapes on the inside of his chest wall. I would have seen the remaining six hairs on the top of his head instantly ping! out of their little follicle sockets and fall to the floor, and I would have seen cartoon bubbles appear above his skull with the words, "Dear God, please save me from this girl!" written inside them.

Uncle Meb said nothing, hoping, I suppose, that I would just forget about it if he ignored me. Boy, was that a wrong assumption. I was nine years old and determined to rid the world of Bad Guys. Besides that, I never forgot anything; I still don't. I inched a little closer and asked louder this time, "What's White Slavery, Uncle Meb?" His newspaper shook again. It took him another thirty seconds before he lowered his newspaper and looked at me somberly.

"I can't explain it," he said. That was all he said. And, from the tone of his voice, I knew better than to press the issue any further. Truthfully, I didn't understand what White Slavery was until I saw the movie, Thoroughly Modern Millie, some fifteen years later. Uncle Meb was right not to tell a nine year old worrywart about the topic. The women in my family would have shot him for that transgression.

Mother relaxed her vigilance a bit as we grew older. For example, she determined (with her X-Ray vision and supersonic hearing, I suppose), that there were no Bad Guys lurking at the Westmoreland Heights Theater near our house. Dean and I were allowed to walk to the Saturday Matinee by ourselves to join a pack of screaming kids.

I can only assume that her relaxed vigilance is why Mother failed to see that her oldest son was fast becoming a Bad Guy - not a *bad* Bad Guy, but more like a thug. He dressed like a hood with his pants riding low on his hips and his hair swooped into various fenders, eagle's asses, and tough-guy configurations. Plus, he had a fast-developing attitude problem, which is why I never got to see much of a movie beyond the Flash Gordon serial.

Invariably, just as the movie began, I was on my hands and knees, crawling around on the sticky theater floor, searching for one of the gold or silver crowns I'd just yanked off my molar while gnawing on a Slo-Poke caramel sucker. After my fourth or fifth trip to the dentist, Mother threatened me with the loss of my life if I ever did this again. But I am a slow learner with a powerful sweet tooth.

So there I was on the floor when the lights went out and an entire squadron of popcorn boxes was hurled at the screen, like bats streaking through the night. Except one. That one would be aimed right at the usher, a surly, pimply-faced teenager who was determined to work his way through college so he could kiss this kind of crappy job good-bye forever. He was ruthless with his bit of power and he hated anyone under the age of sixteen. The popcorn box that nailed the usher was always thrown by my brother. Always. He was a good shot. Up would come the lights. The movie stopped. A huge groan would fill the theater and every child, an entire battalion of snitches, would point accusative fingers at my brother. We were forced to leave the movie theater, thrown out, my head hung down in shame. Even though I never tossed a popcorn box in my life, I had to leave the theater with my popcorn-box-throwing-brother because I wasn't allowed to walk home by myself. Although Mother determined the theater was free from danger, she was sure there were Bad Guys lying in wait between the picture show and our house.

So, other than The Ten Commandments, which we saw every Good Friday at the Jefferson Drive-In for years and years, and whatever other movies Mother took us to, I never saw an entire movie, start to finish, until I was thirteen. That's when Barbara Depew and I lied to her Mother and said we were going to see Thomasina and watched The Carpetbaggers instead. And not for one minute did we worry about Bad Guys. We didn't have to; they were all in the movie.

Although Mother was sure Bad Guys were anywhere and everywhere, only one out of the five of us ever encountered a Bad Guy in real life. He was robbing the gas station I stopped at one night. The Bad Guy demanded my money and because I was twenty three years old and confident of my strength and abilities I grabbed the end of the gun he was pointing at me. He yanked it away and pounded me with it a couple of times, but it's not as though he was lying in wait to get me, which is how Mother described the modus operandi of a truly Bad Guy.

The thing that shocked me most was the smell of blood - raw, fresh, pungent, and almost sweet, like liver. It shot out of my head with each racing heartbeat and splattered against the concrete. Even the grit of oil and dirt and grease grinding into my cheek from the garage floor couldn't distract my nose from that smell - the surprising, ragged odor of my own life squirting out of me.

I just needed some gas and a pee, I thought. *It's nine o'clock at night, too early to be tied up, thrown on the floor, too early to die. To die? I'm too young to die!* Puffed up with inexperience and my own invincibility, I'd rejected Mother's fears and determined for myself the world was a safe place. Because I'd never been robbed and never faced a real gun, I reverted back to childish heroics. Never did I imagine that smarting-off to a robber and grabbing the end of his pistol would make him blam me in the head with his weapon over and over. I never thought he would tie me up and promise to blow my brains out. *It's almost my birthday*, I kept thinking.

Actually, my brain was racing, pumping, and I was horribly fascinated watching a dark red arc of blood form midair before it hit the pavement and splattered across the floor. At the same time I was thinking that all the clocks of my life, all the gears which have turned in my own special universe just for me, were about to grind to a halt - right now - at the whim of a young man who needed my money to help buy a shot of dope more than he needed to understand my refusal to give it to him. I was also tugging at the cord holding my wrists together behind my back and repeating over and over again, "*I'm not going to live to see twenty four.*"

I did survive, obviously, thanks to the grace of God, luck, and my startling newfound ability to untie a knot behind my back faster than anyone would have thought humanly possible. He hurt my hard head, but he didn't kill me. He only killed parts of me - some of the really good parts. And that is a hard thing to know.

Therapy straightens out the fabric of a life, but I don't think anything can ever wash away the smear of getting soundly clobbered or bleach out the humiliating dark spot of begging another human being not to end my life. Such experiences stained the essence of who I was, who I thought I was; and it is a stain that has never gone away. Never again have I felt secure at night. Always I keep my guard up.

All the memories of that one terrifying episode came flooding back to me thirty years later when a young man tried to break into my office on a sunny spring afternoon. I was all alone.

For thirty years I had mentally trained myself for just this occurrence - had promised myself to redeem pride and courage. I heard him out in the hallway and whoooshed open the door to confront him. "Take your screwdriver and scram," I yelled; but I didn't wrestle him to the ground and I didn't gouge his eyes out or make him plead for his life as I had imagined I would for thirty years.

I am much braver and meaner in my imagination than I am in real life, and that too, often feels like its own gray blanket of shame - wet wool riding heavy and smelly across my shoulders.

New memories lay over old memories with crystal clarity - not foggy as I sometimes wish they were, not funny as I often try to make it when I tell the story. I can still smell the smells, even when I don't try; even when I try not to. Only recently have I been able to force myself to stop after dark to buy gas or pop in to a convenience store without thinking someone was there to blast me off the planet. I am still wary and weary of it.

I want to believe that there is more to all of us than just good and evil. I'd like to believe that sometimes when we bounce hard against each other for reasons we can't always explain, we're not really Bad Guys, we are just lost in our desperate feelings of sadness or pain, or longing to feel something different than what we feel. I like to believe I can be big enough to forgive all of it. Maybe I can. Only maybe.

But I think Mother was right. We have to watch out for Bad Guys; we may come across them; and they can hurt us. My highest ideal, though, the one by which I try to live, is that deep within the heart of every Bad Guy is a kernel of integrity that can create a Good Guy. In that is my healing. In that is my hope.

Peggy's Dimpled Smile

"Good things happen when you meet strangers."
- Yo Yo Ma

Chapter 3 – Strangers *(I'm glad I talked to)*

When I was a child, shortly after the earth cooled, back before the phrase "Stranger Danger" had been launched into the vernacular at kindergartens, day schools, elementary schools, and the shopping malls of America, my Mother told us right from the get-go, flat-out, "Don't talk to strangers!" This never made sense to me, though. *How would you ever get to know anybody unless you talked to strangers?* I thought and, *Wasn't everyone a stranger at some point before they became your friend?* I have finally decided, regardless of what Mother thought, sometimes a stranger is the nicest gift you can receive, a God-plop just landing right at your side when you need them. I learned this both the hard way (they showed up when I needed them) and the easy way (I didn't have to ask for them).

My first God-plop stranger incident involved my crummy Corolla, which I bought before Toyota began making really good cars. The first of the cars Toyota shipped over here were not so good. Okay, they were crummy. At least the one I bought, a 1970 Toyota Corolla, was crummy. Actually, crummy is really too nice a description - this car was crappy. I really only bought the thing because my friend Joey said Toyotas had good radios - how smart was that? Anyway, my Corolla was dinky and tinny-sounding and didn't have an air conditioning.

I had to have air conditioning. Remember, I lived in Dallas, Texas. Dallas in the summer was a boiling cavern of heat and humidity. When I picked up the car, I told the dealership to add on an air conditioner. Oh, they did. But because the car was new to Texas, they must not have had factory AC. The unit they bolted onto my little car looked like it could freeze out a Mercury Marquis station wagon. It was way too big for the skimpy little engine in my Corolla. I turned on the

AC once and had to have the car towed in to Mr. Webb's garage. I never turned it on again.

Every part of the car seemed to go haywire at one time or another, but the worst problem was the clutch cable design. It came through the firewall right beside the battery. In very short order, battery acid would eat through the clutch cable and I'd be stuck somewhere, sitting on a curb, trying to figure out what to do.

Seems like I spent a lot of time sitting on curbs with my head in my hands, trying to figure out what to do to get myself out of my latest mess. I was in a lot of messes. Money was tight. Barely an adult in my mid-twenties, I was trying to learn how to make my own way in the world. My apartment was an overpriced roach motel near the airport. I was paying for that crummy car. I worked in rock 'n roll radio. I know there are some people who make really good money working in radio - the stars, I suppose. But if you're a star-maker (like I was) and not the star (like I was not) well, let me just say that you're expected to coast a long way on the fun and excitement of working in broadcasting.

This particular mess happened early one morning on my way to work. The Corolla's clutch cable broke just as I was taking off from a light. The only place my car and I were going was to the curb (I pushed it). Then I got out, raised the hood, and walked across the street to a little diner to look for a pay phone.

I fumbled through my pockets and found enough change to make one call. Luckily my boss was in early that day. He sighed when I told him what happened. "I'll be in as soon as I can, Jim;" I said. "I'm just not sure how I'm going to work this out." Payday was three whole days away and I was already broke. I hung up and rested my head against the phone.

That's when the man sitting at the counter suddenly pivoted on the stool and looked at me with clear light blue eyes. I'd never seen eyes that color before, almost a cornflower blue, and they were exactly the same color as his jacket. His hair was white and combed straight back, receding a little in the front and with a bald spot at the rear. Our eyes met and he smiled.

"I'll help you," he said.

"Okay," I replied. Even as I said the word, I surprised myself. This was so unlike me, so unlike my mother's daughter, so unlike who I knew myself to be. This man drove the two of us for much of the day all around Dallas in his rattling old station wagon. I cannot remember his name; indeed, I may never have known it.

First, he took us over to my mechanic, Mr. Webb. Bless Mr. Webb's sweet old heart. He agreed to line up a tow truck, retrieve my Corolla, provide credit for the new part, fix my car, and wait for me to pay off the whole thing over time. "Your job, young lady," Mr. Webb said; "is to get the parts I need to do the job so I don't have to leave the shop."

My new friend (I'll call him, Mr. Stranger) drawled, "Well, I guess we can do that. I don't have anything else to do." He turned to me and said. "And you don't have anything else you can do until your car is going again."

I couldn't argue with that; so we hopped back into his station wagon to rattle our way across town to the only Toyota dealership in Dallas. I still find it significant that the dealership was located on Lemmon Avenue. We picked up the parts Mr. Webb called in and then turned out of the parking lot to chug our way back across town to Mr. Webb's in South Oak Cliff.

Dallas is a large city and the trip had already burnt up a lot of time. I fidgeted as the worry rose in me. I began to sweat and probably looked pale, like carsickness was imminent. "What's the matter, young lady?" Mr. Stranger asked me.

Now how do you explain to a silver-haired, clear-eyed hero that the big city of Dallas would not be big enough to save me if Mother called work and I wasn't there? *Especially*, I thought, *if she knew a man I'd never seen before in my life was driving me all over Dallas County in a strapped-together station wagon which smelled, oddly enough, like fresh-mown hay. Maybe he buried the bodies of his victims in a pasture or something. Jeepers! Mother would absolutely SHOOT me if I wound up getting myself murdered by a stranger.* Out loud I stumbled and mumbled, "Uhh, Mother, uhh, sometimes she calls ... Jim, my boss, might ... ohh ... if Mother, ohhh ..."

He swung to the curb and pointed to a phone booth. "Thank you," I murmured with heartfelt relief as I tilted my purse to capture any loose coins rolling around the bottom and came up empty. "I'll just be a moment." I patted my pockets. "Really, it won't take long," I dove into my purse again.

"Do you need a quarter for the call?" My new friend offered. It must have been easy to see I was broke, broke, broke.

"Oh, no, no; it's not necessary," I refused. "Thank you, but I'm sure ... just a second, I think I have a ... yes!" With a cry of triumph - just a tad too loud - I pulled a beautiful silver quarter out of the dark purse depths. I was so relieved to reserve a shred of dignity, I practically danced to the phone. "Mother," I kind-of shouted, "my car broke down. It's being towed to Mr. Webb's. I'm not at work. Don't worry." I was talking way too fast. "A very nice man is driving me around to get car parts and stuff. Don't worry."

"What?" she screeched into the phone. "Jody, have you lost your mind?"

"Mother," I said, more calmly than seemed normal for me, "I don't feel afraid. I'll be fine. It's okay." And it really was okay. I was fine. I wasn't afraid. And I couldn't figure out why. I was silent and thinking while we dropped off the parts. The sun bounced off the window all the way from Oak Cliff to my job in downtown Dallas. I stared the leaves on the passing trees. Finally, I turned back to look at him. "Why are you doing all of this for me?" I asked calmly.

He seemed a little shocked, which turned into wistful, then perplexed, and then resigned. He looked at me with those clear blue eyes. "When my daughter was your age," he said, "I was gone a lot."

We drove the rest of the way in silence. Mr. Stranger dropped me off at work. I thanked him for all his help and then he vanished from my life although I never forgot him. Why did our paths cross? Why did it all happened the way it did? Looking back I think he was a sweet man who suddenly had a chance to pull angel duty and took it. For one day, he was my guardian angel.

The next week I found a $20 bill in the pocket of my only jacket. Without a doubt it was from Mr. Stranger - one last blessing.

My second God-plop stranger incident occurred many years later while I was on a do-it-yourself, seat-of-your-pants book tour promoting my novel, <u>The Second Coming of Curly Red</u>. I was traveling on the "red-headed stepchild pass" - also known as a Buddy Pass. This meant the airline wasn't making any money off of me. Basically I was a pain in the neck and everybody on the airplane (except passengers who worked for other airlines) were more important than I was.

New York City was my next stop, but we changed planes in Chicago and that's where I got bumped off my flight. Then bumped again. Then bumped again as did a big guy sitting across from me in the waiting area. His name was Brian Perry and he was trying to get to New York, where he lived with his family in New Hyde Park. Brian worked for Lufthansa Airlines, which made him more bumpable than I. He thought this was funny. I laughed with him, but I didn't think it was funny at all.

Our only chance of getting to New York City was to run from gate to gate and get on each list. Brian was a big, tall man. I am a short, round woman. Together we bounded through the halls of O'Hare airport going as fast as we could from gate to gate. I saw our reflection in a window. We looked like a ball and a bat. But despite our teamwork and best efforts, our names had been taken off all lists. All the flights were full.

One of my more unattractive traits when I get thrown off my game is that I tend to awfulize. I take a difficult situation and imagine it stretched out to its most dreadful possible conclusion; this is awfulizing. I wish it weren't so, but I am good at it.

In my mind I imagined myself wandering the halls of O'Hare airport, smelling like McDonald's grease, rejected by airlines everywhere. Once my money was gone, I'd leave the airport and be reduced to brown-baggin' it with the bums by Lake Michigan. I'd stagger around for as long as I could, then plop down waiting to freeze to death on a park bench, curled up beside a mangy dead dog named Critter. He would be the only pal I had left and we would die together, old, frozen and hairy. And one of the worst parts is none of my friends and family would ever know - or care - what happened to me.

"Yeah," my family members would say to each other, "what ever happened to ol' Jo? She was really starting to show some promise, you know. Remember that book she wrote, whatever it was - that Curly Joe thing? I never read it, but I heard it was good. Yep, real good, that's what I heard. Boy, it was the weirdest thing - she just vanished - poof!"

Then my friends would say, "She must have been talking to strangers or something and they toted her off. I bet that's what happened. You'da thought her Mother woulda warned her about that..."

That's called awfulizing, see? I can wrestle myself into a rotten outcome and doomsday scenario in almost no time at all. But six foot six Brian Perry, my new friend, The Big Stranger, would not let me go to that place in my head. Brian kept me in the moment. He made me laugh; told funny stories about his wife and children.

We both finally wrangled our way onto the last flight out of Chicago to New York. I waved a final good-bye to him as he strolled past my aisle to his seat. We were strangers. We would never see each other again; that's what I thought. But I was wrong. On Saturday night, at a bookstore in the Village, all the way into Manhattan from New Hyde Park, New York, sat the biggest, sweetest guardian angel a girl could ever ask for. He'd probably blush and deny it if I said so, but I know guardian angels surround us almost always, and most of the time they look just like us. And I also know one when I see one. On this particular weekend, mine just happened to be six foot six and wearing glasses. So, you can call him what you want. Me? I call my angel "Brian".

"I arise each morning torn between a desire to
improve the world and a desire to enjoy the
world. This makes it hard to plan the day."
- Author Unknown

Chapter 4 – Atom Bombs and/or Communists

Being children in the 1950's and 60's in Dallas, Texas afforded us all the opportunity to spend lots of time practicing for that fateful day when a nuclear holocaust and all-out showdown with Russia could no longer be avoided. Sooner or later we were just going to have to punch them in their collective Communistic nose; we all knew it.

Seeing as how we had, in the Dallas-Fort Worth area, more than enough defense plants, military bases and right-wing hotheads to make us a major target for any Russian ICBM's, there was no doubt that we'd have to hit them before they hit us. And, most certainly, we could have. Between Carswell Air Force Base, Hensley Field, the Naval Air Station, Texas Instruments, Collins Radio, General Dynamics, and LTV, just to name a few, there was more missile and military know-how in the Dallas-Fort Worth Metroplex than you could shake a warhead at. We just hoped we'd live long enough to get to use it.

It was an era of propaganda, spies, escalation and terror on the international level. At home, it was fallout shelters, doomsday theories, and the stockpiling of non-perishable items. Kids at my school wore Army-style dog tags for easier identification of their charred, gooey remains in the event of a nuclear attack. I still remember the sound and feel of my metal tags clinking against my chest as I rounded third base during a softball game. Once, during a heated tetherball match, my tags flew up and took a tiny chip out of my right front tooth. Another time, while I was playing touch football, they clanged me right in the eye. Staying safe was starting to feel dangerous.

Nothing was deadlier, though, than the blast from an atomic bomb, which, according to Mother was most likely aimed squarely at my fifth grade class at L.O. Donald Elementary School. Our teachers did their best to make us all feel safe, assuring us almost daily that the Communists were not interested in overtaking our own particular elementary school, only the ones in New York, probably, where there were so many more people.

I didn't buy it. I knew better. My mother's children were at this school. My mother hated Communists and even wrote letters to the editor about it. The Reds probably had a file on her already. Therefore, it would stand to reason that our school would be a prime target - simple deduction. Besides, according to Mother, our government couldn't be trusted to do very many things right, so we had to be ready to take matters into our own hands. This was one of two reasons I saved my birthday money to buy a gas mask at the Army-Navy Store. The second reason, of course, was the fact that I was a budding member of the Future Dykes of America, only I didn't know it then. I thought I just liked uniforms.

My U.S. Army-issue gas mask kept me safe for months as I snorked around the house, breathing like an iron lung and looking like an anteater. I kept a notepad and pencil with me at all times, so I could stare out the window through the cataract-like lenses of my gas mask, scanning our neighborhood to check for subversive and/or Communist activity. Perhaps a missile silo was being installed down at the end of our double block.

Eventually, my gas mask began to fall apart - one of the lenses popped out and the hose cracked (so much for government-issue sturdiness), but the real reason I finally quit wearing the thing was because it freaked my baby sister out every time she saw me in it and she screamed loud enough to melt a chunk of Velveeta.

I decided my mother had a firm enough handle on the policing of our off-the-rack, average American neighborhood since she was home every day, so I would concentrate on anti-Communist matters at L.O. Donald Elementary School. I'm sure my teachers were thrilled.

One of the things I remember doing at school was watching a film about the effects of an atomic explosion. Houses blasted apart or burst into flames fueled by horrific winds. The charred imprint of a human body was scorched into the side of a brick building. People who'd been standing right there before the atomic blast were reduced to a pile of ashes and maybe some loose change. I was pretty much steeled against the horror of it, reciting over and over in my head only my name, rank and telephone number: Jody Seay, Texan, oldest daughter of Jo Seay, FE 1-4691.

But this atomic blast movie stuff was hard information for some of my classmates to digest. Anna Lou Perry passed out and Janet Grigsby (not their real names) peed in her pants before the film was over. So many kids were crying that they had to stop the whole thing early. Then our teachers and our principal all assured us that we were perfectly safe and not to worry about anything we'd seen in the film actually happening to us. Just to be sure, though, we were going to begin practicing a new drill.

To ensure our survival from an atomic blast, the U.S. Government instructed the school systems of America to teach a "duck and cover" drill, whereby, America's school children would crouch under their desks, face down and knees up under them, their heads covered with their arms and hands. That is how most of America did this drill. Not at my elementary school. We did it differently.

We filed out into the hallways, making two complete rows of children for each class - one with their heads up against the locker doors, and the second row of kids with their heads up against the feet and butts of the first row of children. Of course, as our science teacher, Mr. Allen, laughingly pointed out, the concussion from an atomic bomb dropped anywhere near Dallas would be so great that the first row of children would have their little skulls firmly implanted into the lockers and those of us unfortunate enough to be on row two would have the unprecedented opportunity to kiss the asses of our classmates a swift good-bye. That's not how he phrased it, but that's what he meant.

I determined that Mr. Allen was probably a Communist sympathizer due to his cavalier attitude about where our heads would wind up in a nuclear explosion. I mean, we had to do something. It wasn't as if our school had access to a fallout shelter. We didn't even have a basement. Mother wanted a fallout shelter at home, though; she lobbied hard for one. We got aluminum siding on our house instead, and I was always rather glad about that. Even though I believed her when she preached about impending doom, atomic blasts and radioactive fallout, I also knew I'd just as soon not be one of the only ones to survive a nuclear holocaust. We'd have to start a brand new country all over again with only my family and maybe a few others scratching around in tainted, luminescent dirt, trying to grow plutonium-flavored onions or something.

Taking on the look of Scarlet O'Hara in front of Tara, my mother's nostrils would flare, and then she would get misty-eyed. I swear violins would be playing <u>America, the Beautiful</u> in the background. No wait...harps! I bet that's what they were - harps played by angels! Flags would wave around behind Mother's head. "If we were the only ones left - just this family - we could rebuild this nation," she would declare, solemnly, as if the Seay family could not only survive a nuclear explosion and subsequent radioactive crop dusting that snuffed everybody else, but we could also manage to find the only ox left on the planet to help us grind up this uranium-tainted dirt and grow ourselves a garden. Why, we could just hook that beast up to the plow we always happened to have handy in the back of our recently cauterized station wagon! No need to worry about the shelf life of our food when we now had half-life on our side! Food would last forever and ever!

Was she kidding? I scoffed to myself, *This family? We can't take a car trip to the Gulf of Mexico without getting pissy enough to shoot each other.* Too much togetherness got on our nerves. Rebuilding a nation was a little beyond what I knew my family to be capable of. But the thought of it kept Mother content, or as close to serene as she ever came in her life. She was, after all, a Republican, and all the Republicans I knew were born to fret.

There was a time when, politically speaking, no greater conservative group of people could be found than your basic Texas Democrats. They were a sturdy group who loved Texas, God and America, in that order. They did not trust businesses or banks or politicians afraid to get dirt on their shoes, or unions, for that matter, who seemed to only want to stir up trouble and shut down plants that were willing to give these hard-working Texans a decent job and a chance at a better life. Then, somewhere toward the end of the 1950's, as the cold war got well into full-swing, a group sprang up in the state of Texas which was so far to the right of everybody else, it made your basic Texas Democrat seem like a Commie Pinko. My mother was part of that group.

Mother never joined the John Birch Society, but she understood why some people did. She thought muckraking Senator Joe McCarthy was a swell guy and that, rather than dying from alcoholism as he did, the liberal media had driven the poor guy over the edge. It never occurred to Mother that people lost jobs and careers and lives after falling under the scrutiny and grinding zeal of Senator McCarthy. No, Mother was certain Hollywood was just crawling with Communists, and that America was skidding fast down a slippery slope, taking all its children toward a godless hell if any liberal stayed in elected political office for too long.

Rather than changing the channel when somebody she couldn't stand was on <u>Meet the Press</u>, and this was usually everybody, she would stare at the television screen, bug-eyed and fierce and with her jaw clenched, muttering under her breath the worst word she ever used, "Bastards."

Mother's politics wrecked her health. I watched her chain-smoke her way to emphysema while writing her daily letters to the editor, most of them urging everyone to IMPEACH EARL WARREN! Of course, in Dallas, in the early '60's, that was like preaching to the choir. The conservative movement was alive, mean and nasty. And it was backed by big business with lots of big money; in fact, not much different than today.

It's shameful that money in large amounts can be used to buy the feelings of and to fool people who want their country to be righteous. I feel the shame of it now even as I write this so many years later. I still remember how closely the hatred in my home town brushed up against me. I did not understand how a city I saw as filled with - mostly - loving people could allow political emotions to ride so close to the surface and allow hatred and anger to boil over. Of course, not all Dallasites felt that way. Not all acted on that anger, but enough did to make the situation ripe, raw and volatile - more than enough.

I campaigned for Nixon in 1960 because my mother was a Republican. But I cheered for Kennedy because somewhere between elections I began to develop a mind of my own. I never told my mother that. There was always something about Richard Nixon that just flat-out gave me the creeps. I never told my mother that, either, but I knew exactly what it was.

During a 1960 campaign stop at Love Field, Richard Nixon shook my hand, sort of. It was a cold night. Maybe his handshake had such a wimpy grip because I was a kid - a girl kid, at that. I don't know; perhaps he was just tired at the end of his fierce campaign. Maybe Richard Nixon would have had a firmer grip if I'd been an Ambassador or Congressman or somebody more important than an eleven-year-old girl with a Texas accent. Nonetheless, I gripped as hard as I could, just like Mother taught me, and there the Vice-President's pasty, sweaty hand lay across my palm like a dead perch.

"Good luck, Mr. Nixon," I said, and he looked at me for just a moment before his eyes darted back and forth. I thought he was trying to figure out which way to run. His face had the same look as our dog whenever she got caught rooting around in the trash. Then he turned away from me and the smile came back on. His arms and hands flew up in the air, and his fingers sprang into the usual V for victory. The crowd cheered wildly, hoping he was the one, hoping he would bring America back to them.

Richard Nixon stood there in the chilly night, hunched, his back bowing out like a question mark, grinning at the crowd like he'd just hit an oil gusher, and all I could think of were my mother's words: "Stand up straight, look people in the eye, and give 'em a firm handshake. And don't ever trust anyone who doesn't do the same."

When President Kennedy was assassinated, Mother was horrified. She hated him, certainly. She didn't want him to be president, but she didn't want him dead, either.

"What has become of us?" Mother said to no one in particular as she sat, hollow-eyed, watching the funeral procession on television. As the rider-less horse, Black Jack, pranced by in the cold autumn wind, jerking the arm of the young soldier who held him, I saw the tears in my mother's eyes begin a slow roll down her cheeks.

My politics and Mother's never really matched after that; although I sometimes pretended they did just to keep her quiet. My politics sloshed around for years, undergoing many incarnations as we slogged our way through the mire of Vietnam and the mess of Watergate. I finally emerged as my family's unapologetic screaming liberal, a position shared by only a few in this rowdy, conservative Texas family. And, yes, in answer to those who think a liberal is a conservative who hasn't been mugged yet, I have been mugged. And I'm still a liberal.

For over thirty years of my life, my mother was certain her children would be slaughtered by atomic bombs and/or Communists, and she did her best to protect us from that. She did not live long enough to see the Soviet Union finally fall over on its side, overspent, worn out and broke. She did not live long enough to see any part of the 1980's "trickle down economics" trickle her way. I made my mother's politics my own as a child because I wanted my mother to love me. I thought I had to agree with her for that to happen. Age has given me the wisdom to know this now as the truth: my mother couldn't have loved me any greater. She just wanted me to vote. And so I do.

"Life is like riding a bicycle. To keep your
balance, you must keep moving."
- Albert Einstein

Chapter 5 – Wheels

In the time before helmets, safety and common sense, I could zip home from my elementary school on my bicycle in exactly three and one half minutes. If I pedaled across the open field by our school like a weasel on speed, cut down the alley where we were never supposed to go, shot out of the alley onto the street and zoomed down the little hill, I'd have enough momentum to propel me halfway up the big hill before I ever had to crank too hard. Then it was a quick left onto the flat part of our street, Glenhaven Boulevard - pump, pump, pump - down another small hill, leaning hard right where the street dog-legged. At this point, going roughly, oh, Olympic luge-competition fast, I'd hit the mound of dirt my brother and I had scooped up by the curb to make a ramp, launch my bike and me into the air like a Titan missile, then crash down with the back wheel only hitting the front walk. If I didn't wipe out when I hit the walk, the last tricky part of this maneuver was to grab the big bottom limb of the mimosa tree, and flip my bike with my legs as it streaked out from under me so it wouldn't crash into Mrs. Shelley's Buick.

Seeing as how I once knocked Mrs. Shelley's side mirror loose when my math book flew out of my basket, I only tried the last part of my bicycle routine on days when I didn't have homework. Mrs. Shelley tended to hold a grudge.

For awhile it seemed that all my focus was on making my bicycle noticed - with handle-grip streamers, a shiny new basket, reflectors, even Mother's canasta cards clothes-pinned just right to fwapada-fwapada-fwapada against the spokes (for which I got into a major amount of trouble). I buffed my chrome fenders until they were gleaming, and put black shoe polish on my tires. My bike and I were shiny, noisy and noticed. And, aside from the time I had a stinger to sternum encounter with a bumble bee who was heading up the street as I was heading down it (causing me to bash myself into the back of the Dunham's '54 Chevy,) my dressed-up bike and I had very few mishaps.

We were definitely a classy couple.

Then I got hooked on speed. No, not amphetamines, silly, but going fast - really fast. An uncle of mine had been a test pilot and I greatly admired his bravery.

As far as I could tell, my Daddy never tried anything new (always Chevrolet cars, Lawn-Boy mowers, and sirloin steaks on Saturday nights), unless you count the year he switched from Falstaff beer to Schlitz, but that wasn't especially brave - or daring. I think maybe it was cheaper.

At any rate, I rather fancied myself as brave and daring - a test pilot of sorts, and I became obsessed with figuring out how fast I could make my bike go. I removed the fenders, the chain guard and snipped the streamers off my grips (too much wind resistance). Then the shiny new basket went (too sissy). Mother made me take her canasta cards off the spokes, apologize, and dig into my birthday stash to help pay for some new ones. This was actually good, however, because even though they certainly made the perfect amount of jet propulsion-type racket, deep down I knew the drag from the cards was holding me back in my quest to break the sound barrier.

Mechanically speaking, I was never quite sure what one had to do with the other, but it seemed to me that as soon as I removed the chain guard from my bike, my chain began going haywire. It would break, or grab me by the sock and not let go, or just flop completely off its sprockets for no apparent reason - throwing a fit, as if it could no longer take whatever punishment I was handing out. Coward.

Once, as I was approaching Mach One, heading into the curve where our street dog-legged, my chain snapped, slapped me hard across my Mary-Jane's, and skidded sparks along the pavement as it broke free and left me altogether. Too late to hit the dirt ramp and save myself by way of the mimosa tree, there was nothing else to do but hang on and head down the double block, which I did, with my mouth wide open, my hair swooshed back like a Smurf doll, and my eyes narrowed into little slits as the G-forces took over.

"Miz Shel111111lleteee!" I screamed as I shot past our neighbor who was out in her front yard with a rake. She looked up, a Kent cigarette stuck between her teeth like a fuse, and then she just waved to me - doodled her fingers at me as if I were strolling past on the sidewalk. Now, I don't know if she was still sulking about the side mirror, but I never thought she did enough to try to save the life of a child obviously out of control and bound for doom. Of course, I'm not sure just what I expected her to do; it's not as if she was some track star who could have flipped her cigarette away, tossed down that rake and sprinted after me. She was no Flo-Jo, and those Kent cigarettes had had their way with her. Also, Mrs. Shelley didn't have access to a jet-propelled anything, as far as I knew, which is what it would have taken to catch me at that point.

The hill was steep, the double-block a long one. I streaked past the Dunham's house, the Underwood's, the Harrison's, gathering momentum, hanging on for life, tears crusted at the corners of my eyes. At the bottom of the hill, the street flattened out a bit. Across from Billy Burdett's house, just before Ronnie Maloney's, I spotted a hedge and aimed my bike for it, praying that it would at least slow me down, praying there were no little kids playing on the other side of it, praying that whoever owned the hedge I was about to crunch would forgive me.

How can I put this? The hedge slowed my bike down; it stopped me more quickly. Emerging from the hedge, scratched and scraped and bloody with shrubbery in my hair, I picked up my battered bike and walked us both back up the long, steep hill. It was just another day in the life of a test pilot.

"It's only a bicycle, Jody, not a jet plane," Mother had said earlier as I smeared Crisco on the frame to cut down on wind drag. "It's never going to break the sound barrier, so you might as well quit trying."

Oh yeah? I would think. *Just wait. Watch this.* And watch is what she did as I dragged my scraped and bruised little self into the house. "My chain broke again," was all I said as I flopped down on the couch. Mother wasn't sympathetic, but she wasn't mad, either. She just sat beside me on the couch with a bottle of Mercurochrome, prodding gently at my cuts and scrapes to make sure nothing needed stitches or a tetanus shot, blowing on my wounds when the medicine stung too much.

"You know, Jody," she said, "Daddy and I have talked about this, and we've decided to go ahead and buy you your very own cannon."

Cannon? I thought, stunned, knowing this was too good to be true, waiting for the other shoe to drop. They wouldn't even let me have a B-B gun the last time I asked, but I hadn't asked in a long time. My very own cannon would certainly be the coolest thing I had ever owned in my young life. Maybe they had both finally come to their senses!

"Yes," she said, "we think a cannon would be just the ticket. You won't have to clobber yourself day after day on your bike. We can just stuff you down the barrel of the cannon and shoot you out of it just about anytime you want. Why, with enough gunpowder, we figure we can blast you all the way up to school. With any luck, and if we aim it just right, you'll only bounce on the black top a couple of times before you hit the bicycle racks;" *har-har-ha*, my mother, the wise guy.

Just a year or so later, my brother Dean decided he wanted a motor scooter or even a motorcycle. He was only twelve and the legal age to drive a scooter then was fourteen, but lobbying in my family for what you wanted took eons. Glaciers would slide off and form subcontinents, or melt and become whole new oceans before your wishes ever came true, so it was best to get an early start. Two year's worth of badgering would be just barely long enough.

"You don't need a goddamned motorcycle," Daddy would say. "I'll just take you out here in the alley and shoot you right in the head. You'll be dead just as quick."

Mother took a different approach. Figuring, appropriately, that the motorcycle was a phase Dean had to go through just like he had to wear engineer boots and leather jackets, she tried to expose him to his dream without actually buying a motorcycle for him. Everything she did was to try and get him through it and past it. Her aim was to keep him alive until he was eighteen and, gosh - who knew - maybe even longer.

Every Saturday after we got back from junior bowling, Mother would leave me at home with the younger kids so we could eat hot-dogs and Jell-O along with Soupy Sales. Then she would lug Dean up to Bill's Cycle Shop and wait in the car for an hour while he straddled each of Bill's motorcycles, fantasizing and going budn-budn-budn until the Harley-Davidson itch deep inside him had been scratched and calmed. Mother was right, too. Her tactic worked, and eventually Dean got over his motorcycle fixation, but, as with most things in my family, it took a really long time.

However, a long time before the fixation was eased, Dean decided he would build a motorcycle, the ramifications of which, I'm sure, he had not entirely thought through. Somehow, he managed to get hold of a motorcycle skeleton. Basically, it was a sturdy metal frame with handle bars, a seat, great big wheels, no brakes, and a place for the motor to ride, should one ever magically appear. It mostly just sat around in the back yard waiting for one of us or the neighbor kids to crawl up on its back, crank its imaginary throttle and pretend to be an important thug of some sort.

This large potential-motorcycle did nothing to add to the quality of adventure in our lives until the day I convinced my brother to pull me down the hill on it and see how fast we could make it go. We dragged it up the street to the top of the hill and tied a thirty foot length of rope from the back fender of his bicycle to the handlebars of this fledgling machine, the almost-motorcycle.

- 43 -

We took off, with Dean pedaling as hard as he could to build up steam. We managed the dogleg onto Keats Drive, gained speed on the down hill (faster-faster-faster) then my tires squealed on our hard left and my molars began to rattle.

I liked going fast, but this was really fast, man. This was cheek-thumping, earsplitting, eye-frying kind of fast, with the wind pounding so hard at my throat, my larynx was about to crack.

I had no brakes to stop me, and no knife to cut the rope between my brother's bike and mine. When I opened my eyes just a slit to peek out, I could see the rope pulled taut as a rubber band, and my brother pedaling away like a trained bear. We were streaking down the street so fast, I thought my hair was about to catch fire! This was doom on wheels, no doubt about it. This was a brain injury just waiting in the wings. This was eating with a mechanical spoon for the rest of my life, drooling on all my relatives and handling blunt objects forever more. I formed the words in the back of my throat and coughed them out against the wind as loud as I could.

"Slow down!!" I screamed at my brother who then hit his brakes and skidded to a stop. I raced past him at approximately the speed of light, with absolutely no way to stop myself until the slack in the rope ran out, which it did. We were suddenly human characters in our very own Road Runner cartoon.

Since the rope was tied to Dean's back fender, as soon as I shot past him, his bike flipped completely up in the air, over his head, and then crashed down on top of him. When my motorcycle contraption and I got to our end of the rope, there was an audible *'sprong'* before that heavy pile of junk on wheels lurched. Momentum slammed me into the handlebars, and then the beast crumpled over on top of me. After a few minutes of wrestling with it, I emerged from beneath the sturdy, and I do mean sturdy, metal frame with a scraped elbow, a torn shirt (with one end of the handlebars sticking out of a buttonhole) and some bruised ribs. Dean had a cut above his ear and tire tracks across the back of his neck. His back fender looked like the horn of a rhino. The pseudo-motorcycle was in perfect shape, however, looking none the worse for wear at all. We gave it to some kid down the street who didn't have an exciting enough life.

Our silent agreement about this was that telling Mother was completely out of the question, which is most often how we handled childhood actions that brought us to the brink of disaster. It wasn't as if we enjoyed having secrets from our mother; we didn't. We all adored Mother. Our silence then, as it would be always with her, was to protect her from the knowledge that she was raising a house full of fools.

A few years later, my cousin Herbie cracked the back of his skull from ear to ear when he wrecked his motorcycle. He was fourteen, on his way back from a Junior High dance and wearing a helmet clearly would have messed up his hair. Herbie walked home from the wreck, puked in the bushes, and then proceeded to jabber like a toddler while his mother raced him to the emergency room. His head swelled up like a basketball and he spent several weeks in the hospital before he got well. From that time on, the mention of yearnings for a motorcycle from anyone in my family drew a terse, one-word response from Mother, "Herbie." It was, and would forever be, enough said.

"How is it that one careless match will start a forest fire, but a whole box won't start a campfire?" - Author Unknown

Chapter 6 – Fire

I became claustrophobic the year my brother Dean and I set the woods on fire. Both of those things were mostly accidental. Our excuse for the fiery and particularly dangerous form of stupidity was that we were young (ages five and six) - and we were, well, dumb. That is a decent excuse. Too bad we were not smart enough at the time to have used it.

It all started with our birthdays. We received nifty rain slickers and boots. After that, we needed very little rationalization to put them on and parade around pretending to be grownups who were brave and important. Mainly, our new outfits just made us sweat. Texas was in the middle of another of its dry spells and the sky hadn't let go of a good spew of rain since the storm that bent the TV antenna pole across the top of our house like a giant pipe cleaner and blasted the stained glass windows out at church.

Dean swiped a book of matches from the off-limits-drawer in the kitchen and decided we should play "firemen". Firemen were obviously brave and important. We had most of the gear we needed: slickers and rain boots. But we did not have a hose that would stretch as far as we needed it to go. *Ah, what the heck?* We thought. *We are brave and true and important-looking.* We were stupid little kids so we took our contraband book of matches and headed to the woods next to our house.

My brother's job, since he had a penchant for pyromania, was to set little poofy tufts of grass on fire. My job, one that would prove to be beyond my fire-fighting capabilities, was to dash over in my slicker and rain boots and stomp them out. It was a system that worked pretty well until I decided that the fireman's job didn't feel very hard to do after all. To liven up the job, I decided to let the little tufts of grass burn just a bit longer; that would make me braver.

Well. Then, without warning (as fire is known to do) the flame from one poofy tuft shot straight up my pants leg. I screamed like the scaredy-cat I knew I was and jumped away, slapping at my smoldering britches. Then, well, then all hell broke loose and we had ourselves a regular forest fire within just a matter of seconds. Slapping, stomping and squealing was no longer going to get the job done. Firemen's work suddenly looked *very* hard to do.

Dean and I scurried like rodents up and down the hill from the woods to our house lugging water in anything we could find: our wagon, a bucket out of the sand pile, the dog's water dish. *"Please, oh please,"* we prayed the whole time we were shuttling water, *"please don't let Mother glance out the window and see the smoke."* That ominous cloud, black, noxious, and roiling, was now billowing up over the woods and across the yard as if a P-51 fighter had just crash-landed by our swing set.

Spotting an old enamel tea kettle Mother used as a planter by the porch, I yanked the plant out, filled the thing with water and took off down the hill. Unfortunately, in my young-ness, I did not understand the dynamics of a planter: there are holes knocked in the bottom of planters, *on purpose,* to allow for water drainage. And, unfortunately, in my dumb-ness, I didn't figure out the repercussions of holes in my pot until my fourth or fifth trip down the hill. Those holes were the reason I only had maybe half a cup of water to fling at this inferno each time I arrived at its edge.

Well. The Palestine Volunteer Fire Department arrived in time to save us all from disaster, but not in time to save my brother and me from the wrath of Mother. By this time, Mother's wrath was considerable, super-sonic, even, and revved to a whine and intensity for the lives of her children and embarrassment at what those same dumb children had done. Her anger was potent. Mother was high-pissed. And we were in trouble.

When she found me, I was racing around in circles like a loony bird, flapping my arms wildly and yelling something like, "What a big mistake! Ha, ha, ha! What a big mistake!" My face was streaked with soot and sweat, my hair was singed, my pants were scorched and, in fact, still smoking, and the ends of my rain boots had melted into two long, pointed and flappy things. They looked almost like flippers or shiny black garden spades.

Before I knew that Mother was near, she had Dean snared by the collar of his slicker and she grabbed my little soda-straw arm. "In the house," she snarled, "both of you, right now!" She looked scarier than I ever remembered seeing her.

Trying to talk our way out of this one just isn't going to work, I thought. *We're screwed; I know it.*

We were grounded, confined to our rooms for a week, which was the worst that could happen to children who were used to playing outside all the time. *But,* I thought to myself, *it's not nearly as bad as being confined to a Home for Wayward Children, Especially Those Beyond Hope, which is where I thought she'd pack us off to.*

We were allowed out of our rooms to sit at the table to eat, but we hunkered over our food like prisoners at San Quentin, tentative, saying little and hardly being spoken to. Our eyeballs *da-bink, da-bink, da-binked* back and forth like tennis balls from our mother to each other trying to gauge just how badly we had screwed up the entire rest of our lives. If there really was such a thing as a permanent record, this would definitely be on it. This was permanent record material, for sure. We knew this because Mother's eyes were still blazing, so the less said, the better. She was still on the shaky side of forgiveness and wasn't going to let go of this little old forest fire transgression for a good long while, nosirreebob, we could tell. Maybe by the time I was ready for college, but not any time soon. Nope. Wasn't going to happen.

By the third day of confinement, I'd read everything I could read, which, given that I'd not started school yet, was not much. I'd colored all the pictures in every coloring book and skimmed through an entire stack of *National Geographic* magazines (I was good at figuring out what was going on from the pictures). After that, I rearranged my bedroom furniture, taught myself how to tie a hangman's noose using shoe strings from which I suspended three of my brother's plastic army men, and built a fort out of my toy box, pillows, socks and underwear drawer, and a piece of cardboard I had stashed under my bed.

I was bored.

When I went to ask Mother if, perhaps, we could renegotiate the terms of our agreement, her head jutted out at me like a snapping turtle. Her message was terse. "No!" was all she said and she pointed down the hall toward my room, my own little jail cell, which is what it had become for me.

They say that hell hath no fury like a woman scorned, but I can tell you a woman scorned can't hold a blowtorch to the fury of a bored Scorpio, over-penalized five-year-old. I stomped down the hall taking off my T-shirt (although I don't know why) and muttering really bad thoughts about my mother out loud, bad enough to get me shipped off to an orphanage if she'd heard them. I whipped my T-shirt up over my head in one motion, but it got hung on my big skull. Suddenly both of my arms were trapped up over my head and the T-shirt covered my face. I staggered around my room with my head and my arms stuck, bellowing like a wildebeest before finally falling over sideways into my closet.

After an eternity of struggling with this straight jacket, I finally emerged from the pile of shoes and toys a changed child. I was just as mad as always, maybe even more so, only now I was also claustrophobic - and have been ever since.

A need rose in me, a need to have the final say in this show-down with my mother. I stood on my bed and wrote on my recently-painted bedroom wall with a big blue Crayola. I wrote the two worst words I could almost spell: DO-DO and CARP. I'm sure there was punishment for this transgression. I may have been confined to my room until my birthday the next year or at least until I'd learned to spell better.

When I think back on it, the fact that we only had two major episodes with fire over the course of our childhood is actually rather a shock. Everyone in my entire clan smoked except my grandmother, all of them puffing away like little choo-choos. There was always an abundance of fire-producing material within easy reach. Daddy carried a four-pound Zippo lighter around in his pants pocket. Mother was big on kitchen matches that could strike up a flame like a torch with little effort just in case she was suddenly seized with an urge to storm the Bastille or something.

A few years later, after we moved back to Dallas, my five-year old brother Mike came crying and jabbering into the living room. He was in hysterics. "It sounds like he's saying, 'The shirt's on fire,'" Dean said, and, sure enough at that instant, thick black smoke came roiling through the house, choking us all as we ran around and into each other trying to figure out what to do. While attempting to light a candy cigarette with Daddy's Zippo, Mike had set the closet in his room on fire.

Although the fire itself didn't destroy very much, smoke from the melting plastic record player in the top of the closet really made a mess of things. Water from the fire department's hoses didn't help a lot, either. Other than actually putting out the fire, I mean. No disrespect intended to those guys, but they sure waterlogged the back of the house to put out such a dinky flame. But I bet their rain boots didn't melt and stretch all out like salt water taffy while they were fire-fighting, either. I'll bet their boots didn't look like a pixie's shoes that had lost their curl.

In this trial by fire that is my life, it is fascinating to me the things we choose to save when we think they might be lost forever. In my life now I would save my picture box, love letters and stories that I've written. These precious things I might not be able to recreate. But back when I was living through that second fire, I chose differently. I tried to save my brother's lizard, the bride doll off my bed and the football. I know the last two seem an incongruous pairing, but I was almost nine years old by the time of the second fire and it was my first identity crisis. Trust me - that's a whole `nother story.

Mother finally forgave Dean and me for the forest fire some time before I graduated from high school, although she never, ever forgot it, not ever! Even after we were adults, a strange look of horror would shadow across her eyes whenever any of us struck a match, like she could see into the future and past all at once - like she could see some picture of her children all crisp and smoldering.

My brother's lizard has been gone now for so many years he's probably already reincarnated as an iguana and ready for his second or third trip through time. My picture box, complete with love letters, stays practically chained to my ankle so attached am I to the sweet photographs of my family and friends and to the wonderful memories they provide. My stories I fear I'd be unable to recreate, I finally put on a diskette and it stays in my purse. I would glue it to my chest if I thought it would make it any safer.

My brother got over his penchant for pyromania, and I got over any silly visions I might have had of emulating my bride doll - sitting primly on the bed in a scratchy long gown, awaiting my Prince Charming. Some things change. And some things never do.

That's why I say, and you can take this one to the bank, that if my house today suddenly went up in flames and I had to dash out with nothing on but my underpants. I'd still make a grab for the football. But the bride doll? Nuh-uh. Nope, sorry. That old gal would be a goner.

*"People get so in the habit of worry that if you
save them from drowning and put them on bank
to dry in the sun with hot chocolate and muffins,
they wonder whether they are catching cold."*
- John Jay Chapman

Chapter 7 – Water

The only thing worse than drowning, I think, is to drown with
your mother only a few feet away from you while you were doing it.
This happened to me twice in my younger life and both times my
mother was right there, chattering away with someone and puffing on a
cigarette. How she managed to keep a cigarette going continuously in
the water is beyond me. Maybe it was practice that gave her the skill,
given that one of us was always going under for the third time (okay,
okay, it was mostly me - not entirely - but mostly). One of us would
often be *glug-glug-glugging* our way toward the bottom of some pool
or creek or lake or swimming hole and Mother would fish us out and
shake us off, never once losing (or even dampening, really) her
Tareyton 100. This ability of hers to maintain a constantly dry smoke
was a true talent, now that I think of it, one that would be her undoing
in the long run.

I was seven the first time I almost drowned. It was at Lake
Palestine on a clear, bright day of a hot Texas summer. We'd already
moved to Dallas, but had returned on vacation to visit friends, Web and
Maureen Bratz, and their three sons.

Our twins were four and stayed constantly in bright orange life
jackets that, consequently, made them pretty indestructible since they
were easy to spot and a cinch to catch if the current wasn't too strong.
They just bobbed along on the surface of the water like little burr-
headed fishing corks.

Dean, my older brother was born knowing how to swim faster than a motorboat. He was quick as a trout and as big and strong as a sturgeon. He could go anywhere in the water, gliding along the surface like a porpoise, cutting through waves with ease and grace. Even at the age of eight, his strength in the water was astonishing.

I tended to sink. Still do. I don't know why. Despite the fact that fat (which I now have in abundance) floats and muscle (which I mostly had as a child) sinks, put me in a swimsuit, sister, and I'm an anvil in Lycra. Bombs Away! Da-boosh! I am a depth charge with wavy hair, able to sink a sub should one happen by. Good for me that I can hold my breath.

I think my bones are too thick or something, like a Charolais cow. Hey, I bet that's it! I was a big ol' thick-boned, curly-headed Charolais heifer in a past life and now I'm having to work out some nasty bovine karma this time around using my square, sturdy teeth and a sad-sounding moo. Or, perhaps I am descended from catfish, a secretive and suspicious bottom-feeder mulling around in the murkiness, avoiding the light, looking for discarded morsels and some loose change.

Despite expert swimming lessons, which I took three times, staying on the surface of the water for any length of time - say, for example, until the Coast Guard shows up to rescue us all from shark-infested waters - eludes me. And it always has. My muscular, bronzed and Coppertone-glazed swimming teacher smiled her thin, stretched smile each time she awarded me my Certificate of Completion, congratulating me with a pruney brown hand on my shoulder. But her head would shake slightly, palsy-like, as she stared at my mother with an intense and stricken warning. That Mom-to-Mom stare said, "Don't encourage this - move to the desert where there is no water or to the mountains where it's too cold to swim - never buy her another swimsuit - this kid sinks like a stone - do something else, anything, but not this!"

Mother didn't believe in the warning. She thought that with gentle and consistent encouragement from her, or, at least, by being constantly dared by my brother, I could put my innate stubbornness and dogged determination to proper use. "Why, before long," Mother was certain "Jody will be skimming along the top of the water just as fleet as a sailfish, rather than scraping her chin and ribs on the concrete or rocks and gravel below." I never skimmed like a sailfish - a catfish, maybe. And, since the bottom was often where I wound up, my brother usually positioned himself close enough to yank me up from the depths before I blacked out.

But not so on this day. No, on this day Dean was out some fifty yards from the shore, diving off a big wooden platform, swimming with strong arms, splashing and playing, then pulling himself back up on the float to do it again. The twins were running and squealing along the shoreline in their bright orange life jackets, flinging themselves over and over into the lake, darting around like tadpoles. Daddy and Web were sitting on the dock, which jutted a few yards out into the lake, laughing at Mother and Maureen who were talking silly while floating back and forth past them on inner tubes. I don't know what the subject was, but it sure was funny to them. Mother would say the words, "sailor" and "how much?" then peels of laughter would ring out from the four of them.

The grownups didn't look so very far away to me, which is why I decided to just walk right out there into the water and join them in their fun. Having determined that only sissies and little bitty kids needed to wear life jackets, I took mine off and stashed it by a tree.

I entered the lake. The sandy lake bottom seemed to head almost straight down and the water was over my head in an instant - way too fast for me to scramble back out of there like a crab or to even yell for help without filling my mouth up with water. Panic-stricken, I flailed away frantically at the soft sand and mud with my feet, like I was riding a stationery bicycle under water, but I only succeeded in digging a hole deeper and deeper. I kicked forcefully at the water - one big, forceful, manly kind of kick like I'd seen Lloyd Bridges do on Sea Hunt - on the off chance that some miracle had happened for me in the swimming technique department and I'd suddenly be able to propel myself completely up and out of the water, landing (ta-poink!) safely right beside our picnic basket on the shore. It didn't work. Like I said, I tend to sink.

After going under, oh, seven or eight times, I felt a momentary sense of joy since I'd always heard people die after they go under for the third time and I was still alive. But the joy was nothing I could smile about without drowning. I was in a fix.

Nobody else seemed to be noticing my fix. Each time I kicked myself upward, I caught glimpses of my parents laughing and yukking it up with their friends on the dock. Once, Daddy was leaning way, way out over the water holding his Zippo up to the tip of Mother's Tareyton. I could see the white of his hiney where his trunks slipped below the tan line on his back. The next trip upward, the one I thought would be my last, my mother was leaning back in her inner tube holding her cigarette between the fingers of one hand and swishing at the lake with her free hand. Her feet kicked lazily at the water and her toenails were the same shade of red as her lipstick. She was laughing and beautiful in her sleek black swimsuit, slightly sunburned across the freckles on her neck and shoulders. Her head was thrown back as she laughed and sunlight glinted off the tips of her cat-eye sunglasses.

The weight of the water crushed against my chest and I felt achingly tired. *This is the last time I'll see he*r, I thought and then, *I'm going to die now*. And just as I got okay with it, just as I felt myself let go and stop the struggle, two strong hands clutched me right around the ribcage from the back and we shot straight up out of the water like a whale breaking the surface. Water spewed out of my lungs and mouth like Moby Dick. Twelve-year-old Kenneth Bratz, heading back down the trail from the car to the lake had seen me struggling. He dove in, pushed me up and out of the water and saved my life, simple as that. I think all the grownups just thought we were playing.

The incident was horrifying to me and I never told Mother. As far as I can tell, Kenneth Bratz never mentioned this incident to anyone, either. I'll admit one of my reasons for keeping quiet is I didn't want to have to wear one of those dorky-looking life jackets again. But I also wonder if there were some incidents that just could not be voiced in our family. For my mother, the horror, shame and guilt over losing one of her children while she was busy pretending to be a hooker on an inner tube would definitely have been one of them. She would never have recovered.

Of course, the next time I almost drowned, later that same summer, Mother and I both chalked it up to my own stupidity. And, truthfully, it happened because of my inability to turn down a dare of any sort, particularly if my bravery was in question. We were at a big swimming pool we didn't usually visit. The pool had a tall slide, a big treat for us since our own neighborhood pool had only the basics: chlorinated water, one Life Guard, a high and low diving board, and hardly any baby doo-doo floating randomly about. But it had no slide. Having a slide to whip down at warp speed was a definite plus. Dean was headed up the ladder before you could say Johnny Weissmuller. He zipped down the slide a few times and then headed for the high board.

I wanted desperately to go down the slide, to prove myself. The only problem for me was my height. Okay, I was short. And the water at the bottom of the slide where I was to splash down was four feet deep, exactly how tall I was. After some quick calculations in my head, I surmised that significant parts needed to keep me alive would be below the surface of the water. I'd have to scramble out of there fast, but given my past track record, well, drowning was practically a sure thing. I couldn't let that slow me down.

Mother was way ahead of me. She grabbed me by the wrist as I pulled and strained to start up the ladder. "Do not," she said, slowly and fiercely, "go down that slide until I am watching you so I can catch you. Do you understand me?"

I nodded my head because I truly did understand her, truly I did, it's just that, well, a lot of things she warned us about turned out to be not such a big deal, and, besides, I had to hurry to get in line with the other fifty kids. I wrenched myself free from her grasp and headed up the wet metal rungs.

Courage is important to me and I have always liked to think I have more of it than I actually do possess. So, despite my terror of heights, I had made it to the top of the giant slide and was set to scoot my shivering little butt down it. Dutifully I scanned the pool area below for my mother. Although this took only a few seconds, the children below were getting restless.

"Go on!" the boy on the second rung said and poked at my back with his finger.

"Stop it!" I snarled, swiping at him with my hand and losing sight of Mother in the process. Then I had to start my search for her all over again. When my eyes finally zeroed in on her, she was chattering away with another Mom, as usual. She was standing there in her black swimsuit and her cat-eye sunglasses, as usual, holding onto a smoldering Tareyton, as usual. She could not have gotten away with smoking in the pool in this day and age, and she would have left if anybody had told her to put her cigarette out or get out of the pool, but back then smoking was okay - whenever and wherever. I don't doubt that Mother could have and would have fired one up while being wheeled into the O.R. for lung surgery, so close and devoted did she feel to the tobacco industry at that point in her life. I could see Mother; she did not see me - standing and shivering at the top of the slide screaming at her, "Motherrrrrrr! Motherrrrrrrr!" She did not hear me over the shrill roar of a swimming pool full of exuberant children, nor did she seem interested in stopping her conversation, and she never even looked up at the top of the slide where I was - me, blue in the face and screaming at her, over and over, "Motherrrrrr!" as the throngs of children up and down the slide, in and out of the pool, began to taunt me in their sing-song way.

"Chicken on the sliiiiiii-iiiide, chicken on the sliiiiiii-iiiide," they sang out until I felt my neck stiffen and resolve settle itself through my gut. It was clear I had no choice. Doom or not, I had to go.

I turned briefly to the boy behind me on the ladder who was leading this taunting torture and thumbed my nose at him. Then I shoved off, racing down the slippery metal slide as if I had just perfected the luge technique. I hit the water right in front of Mother like a log headed to the mill. I bobbed to the surface only once before I sank back under and began to glug-glug-glug. I held my breath awaiting death or for the sudden, violent explosion of my lungs. What I felt instead was instant upward propulsion as I rocketed toward the sky. Mother had spotted me, lunged under, grabbed me by the hair and pulled me up and out of the water where I clung to her like a baby baboon. Her Tareyton was between her lips, still lit, but soaked, and limp as a two-week-old carrot. She snatched it out of her mouth with two fingers and flipped it completely over the fence in one quick motion.

Mother seemed mad, but I couldn't tell if it was because I'd splashed her so badly or that her cigarette was wrecked or that I'd almost drowned right there in front of her while she was busy chatting. "You were supposed to wait until I saw you," she said as she held me and carried me over to the edge of the pool where our towels were. There was anger in her voice. Then it softened, and she pulled my head in closer to her neck. "You were supposed to wait until I saw you." She sat me on the edge of the pool and wrapped her beach towel around me.

"I know," I said.

"This water is over your head, Jody."

"I know."

"You could have drowned."

"I know."

"Then why didn't you wait?"

"The kids were calling me 'chicken,' Mother. I had to go."

"Do you have to take every dare?"

"Yes, ma'am," I said, wiping at my runny nose with the edge of her towel. "I do."

Mother ran her fingers across my quivering blue lips and looked deeply into my little bloodshot eyes. I almost saw a smile behind her hazel ones. I shivered as she rubbed the towel over my head, and tightened it around my shoulders. She nodded her head, finally, in agreement. "I know," was all she said, just, "I know."

"You don't drown by falling in the water; you drown by staying there." - Edwin Louis Coles

Chapter 8 – Water Everywhere

Of course, since there was such a big mess of us (Mother's children, I mean), I was not the only one to nearly drown; I was just the one who seemed to do it most often. Nor was I the only one to almost buy the farm while exhibiting a tremendous amount of bad judgment and/or stupidity. Certainly the law of averages would catch up with each of us at some point. And, seeing as how I am equal opportunity writer, I feel it my duty to point out the shortcomings of my siblings so my readers won't wonder why I wasn't just tossed off a cliff right from the start so everybody else could get on with their lives.

As I recall, my brother Mike stepped in a hole at the lake and chugged under before Mother could even start screaming. A teenage girl sitting on the bank flirting with her boyfriend dove in and pulled him up so fast that her ratted hairdo, sprayed as stiff as a Tupperware bowl, didn't even get completely soaked through. The whole thing took less than a minute and it was astonishing, like watching a cartoon. Mike glugged under, the young woman stood, dove in, and yanked Mike up onto the shore like a tuna. Then she just climbed right back up on that bank and continued to flirt with her fella - mascara running down her cheeks - like nothing unusual had just taken place. What a trouper! It transpired so quickly, we didn't have time to get to Mike or to even get very scared about what had just happened. He sank, she saved him, and life went on - boom - just like that. All Mother could think of to do was invite the girl over to our campsite for hot dogs.

Unlike most of the familial near-death experiences I have shared with my siblings, this was one for the record books in the sheer efficiency of it, if nothing else. Time seemed to stand still. The memory of it burnt into my brain, as enduring as a cattle brand. There were more incidences, too.

As adolescents, both my younger brothers dove off the back of a speeding motor boat to grab and swim back with our sister, whose ski belt had just unhooked and whooshed away in the wind. That was the same summer my brother Dean, the thug, saved Don Hendrickson, the preppie quarterback of our varsity football team, from drowning at Lake Texoma. I remember how Dean's stomach was shaking, vibrating, as he dragged his friend out of the water and up onto the dock. He pulled him halfway across the cove. My brother, the badass, was always the hero.

The one I remember most, however, was the one where I actually participated in the save. It happened at Turner Falls. Turner Falls is one of the many magical sites in Oklahoma. Mother tended to cast a wary eye on the state of Oklahoma since it is north of Texas and was, therefore, a potential hide-out for "Yankees". The memories bubble up and surface: hot day, late August, Mother, grandmother (Mama Loyes) and a picnic. If we were brave enough, we could dive off the falls and we could have our pictures taken on the same big rock where our mother and grandmother had posed when each was a teenager. Dean was thirteen, I was twelve, the twins, Pat and Mike, were nine, and Peggy, our baby sister, had just turned four. The year was 1962.

We all swam and played in the cool water, letting the spray and shimmering mist engulf us on this summer day. Mama Loyes, whose idea of "swimming" was an abbreviated dog-paddle, got dunked more than once and was an amazingly good sport about it. Then Dean and I raced each other up the side of the cliff to a foothold about halfway up the falls and dared each other to jump first. Well, the result was I did a body-slam of a belly-flop into the drink so hard it knocked the wind out of me, turned my thighs and chest bright red for a couple of weeks, and imprinted the words JANTZEN spelled backwards across the bottom of my ribcage which didn't fade until I was almost through Junior High School.

Mother tossed Peggy over to Mama Loyes and swam out to make sure I wasn't about to heave up my innards. She stood there with her arm around me as I wheezed and hacked and caught my breath. We both watched Dean make a big fart noise with his armpit, then turn and sail out from the rocks and straight down beside the falls in a dive as clean and thrilling as one of those guys who dived off the cliffs in Acapulco. My brother was amazing.

Some time later, after we were all sufficiently Coppertoned, sunburned and waterlogged, Mother and Mama Loyes took Peggy and headed back down the creek toward our picnic area. "Don't do anything stupid," Mother cautioned us over her shoulder. "And be no later than 15 minutes behind us."

Well, I thought, "*Who has a watch?*" Out loud I whispered to Dean, "Don't do anything stupid?" We chuckled. "Hey, that's what we're known for - danger and stupidity."

We piddled and dawdled, of course. There was a major moss fight under a big tree until a leech stuck itself to my neck. This created more havoc and girl-like behavior than I am proud to speak of. I jumped around like a Watusi warrior and screamed like a banshee before Dean finally pulled it off me. He called me a sissy (a name that burned like acid in the pit of my stomach, I don't mind telling you,) and took Mike with him further downstream.

Pat stayed with me. We came to a very wide and deep spot in the creek and Pat, in a moment of misguided courage, decided to swim across the whole thing, and I was to pull him out if anything went wrong. *Oh boy.*

Pat swam across to the other side with no problem. He crawled up on the bank and waved to me before diving back in. When he was right in the middle, right at the deepest part where the water was over his head and mine, his leg cramped and he yelled before his head sank under the water. A second later he popped up, his eyes were wild and terrified. "Jody, I can't make it," was all he said before I heard that all-too-familiar glug-glug-glugging noise. And then he started to sink.

I couldn't think of anything else to do; so I dove in and swam under him. The water at this point was over my head, but not by much.

Luckily for us both, I could hold my breath for extended periods of time before losing consciousness. I surfaced once, took in a big slug of air, then dove back under and positioned myself directly below my floundering little brother. I got a pretty firm foothold on the gravely bottom of the creek, put my hands on Pat's ribcage, pushed my arms straight up as high as they would go and lifted him out of the water so that he wouldn't drown. It worked. However, it was easy to see we wouldn't be able to do this forever.

Of course, it never occurred to me to just turn to my left and, still holding Pat above me, just walk toward the shore where seven or eight steps would have taken us out of the danger zone. Nope, in my panic, we stayed right there, right in the deepest part, only a gasp or two away from doom. Clearly, we were in a pickle.

I needed to think. Fortunately, when you're holding your breath under water, there's not much of anything else you can do. As I was thinking and Pat was kicking and flailing above me, I opened my eyes and could see through the clear water waaaaaaaayy down the creek. There were the long, strong, very sunburned legs of my older brother walking slowly along. My lungs were beginning to ache and terrible thoughts swam around my head. *What kind of man would my brother Pat have grown up to be, had he lived, God bless him,* This thought scared me, was too comfortable to bear, it was a thought too easy to give in to. I let go of Pat and kicked my way to the surface and screamed, "DEEEEEEEEEEEEEEEEEAN!!" with all the force in me as soon as I saw sunlight. Then I quickly dove back under Pat and lifted him out of the jaws of death.

And, speaking of jaws, my brother Dean came at us like a shark, fast and powerful; I could see him under the water. He was a human PT boat swimming upstream; a torpedo in swim trunks. His legs were kicking like Tarzan's when Boy was about to go over the waterfall on the giant lily pad and Tarzan had to save him. The force of Dean formed a cyclone of water and energy that lifted all three of us straight up into the air. I was the first to fall from it, but managed to keep my head above water. What I saw that day I will remember for the rest of my days. When I am very old and can't remember where my underpants are, what pills I have to take, or where I left the pot roast, I will remember this.

Dean and Pat were suspended in mid-air, held up by something bigger than the three of us combined, probably the spirit of every child who'd been entrusted with the care of a younger sibling and almost blew it. Anyway, it was big, really big, whatever it was. Dean lifted Pat up by the ribs, gave him a shake and yelled at him, "I told you to stay out of the deep water!" Then, in a display of strength I haven't seen in a thirteen year old since, Dean threw our little brother completely over the top of the water to the bank which was fifteen or twenty feet away. With a soggy-bagpipe-type of thud, Pat landed on the sandy and gravely shore like a carp.

It would not be fair to say we never wanted Mother to know when we were hurt or wounded. Indeed, any extra attention we could get via a cut or scrape, twisted knee or broken bone was always welcomed and we lapped it up like kittens with cream. But a near-demise was a whole different dog and the bond created between us by our silence when one of us had nearly been snuffed was stronger than any need for extra attention. Besides, if she'd known all the close calls we'd had, she would never have let us out of the house, not ever, nosirrebob. Jo Seay would have raised the drawbridge and that, as they say, would have been that. We'd all still be there, at home, in the den, a pack of embittered, middle-aged titty-babies, playing cutthroat canasta and bitching about how we were never even allowed to get close to the edge of courage or to scrape up against the faces of our own dragons. And Mother, as much as she loved us, as much as she hated the thought of any of us hurt or killed, and as much as she fought all our lives to keep us safe - well, Mother would have hated that more than anything.

"One drink is too many for me and a thousand is not enough." - Brendan F. Behan

Chapter 9 – Firewater (*and not a drop to drink*)

For twenty years I drank too much. *Waaaaaaaaayyy* too much if you want to know the truth, which is what I aim to tell here. Actually, there are people in the world who don't drink - never have - don't intend to. Well, I drank my share and theirs, too, so I guess somebody's having a whing-ding of a time these days on what was left of my share because I gave it up in 1988 and never looked back.

Even when I quit, I didn't quit because I drank too much, nope, not at all. That part never occurred to me. I quit drinking because I wanted to quit smoking. I was wise enough to know if I drank alcohol, I'd want a cigarette. I wasn't wise enough to know my liver was probably swollen up to the size of a toaster-oven at that point. The fact that my liver-lobes and I can now pass a liver function test without looking as yellow as a rutabaga is really just a lucky accident.

It is impossible to figure out where the alcoholic gene came from on either side of the family, even though, Lord knows we'd all like to have somebody to blame it on. What little chink in the double helix of our collective DNA matter caused my drinking fiasco? What was the name of the first of my knuckle-dragging relatives to slurp down a gallon of mushy berries left too long on the vine in the sun? Which ancestor thought to ingest fruit that had been peed on by bears, puked up by coyotes, and rotted into a sticky, potentially intoxicating, wine-smelling mess? In my mind, I can see this ancestor (I look very much like him, only I am cuter, I think; I hope). Yes, I can see him belch loudly, pat his pelt-covered belly, gurgle, "*Urgh!*" and pass out in the back seat of a Buick - uh, no - make that in the back of the cave. *Ahhh, it's always good coming home!*

Mother never warned us about alcohol, but she should have. I used to wonder why she didn't, but now I figure it was because she would've had to name names, as in, "...Well, you don't want to wind up like old Uncle Cirrhosis there, the only one to actually go to sleep *before* Thanksgiving dinner..." She might have hurt somebody's feelings, might have destroyed a fantasy or two, and might have pissed somebody off. Mostly, it would have taken up a lot of time, since we had a startling number of alcoholics staggering toward, stumbling away from, leaning up against, passed out below, and dangling from our family tree. On our family's coat of arms (if we'd had one, which we didn't) would have been a branding iron, a horseshoe, a bowling ball and a beer bottle. We were Texans through and through.

My partner Stef is an amazing woman, and the most brilliant schoolteacher I've ever seen. As I listen to her tell the stories of her life, I am in awe of the things she did, the things she survived, before she got married and had three kids: driving twice across North Africa, getting caught in the war in Beirut, dumped off a Russian freighter in Alexandria, kayaking for three months from Vancouver, British Columbia to Juneau, Alaska, crewing on a sailboat from Canada to Mexico, and boating one thousand miles down the Yukon River. The list of thrills and dangers and courage it all took seems endless.

After telling another friend about Stef's adventures, she said, "So, does that make your life seem pretty dull by comparison?"

"Well," I said, "I had some exciting times - dangerous, even - in my younger years; it's just that they usually involved a tremendous amount of alcohol, often a speeding car, along with some smelly hitchhiker we'd befriended, and my cousin Herbie who, even though I knew he loved me, seemed determined to get us both killed." I can remember big chunks of almost all of it and there is not much I am proud of (like the alcohol and the speeding car part). This is the truth, tangled up in the lint trap of who I am today, with all my joys and wrinkles and regrets, and with all of the other strings and straws and wires of my life.

My Uncle George was a sad but good-hearted man, as sweet as the cheap wine he always smelled of. He walked, sometimes stumbled, around the tiny country town where he lived whistling <u>Alabama Jubilee</u> and never anything but that. He was the youngest of my grandmother's siblings, the baby brother whom they all coddled and adored. But no one really expected a lot from him, especially when it became clear Uncle George just didn't have a lot to deliver, responsibility-wise.

Uncle George was the first to die of that bunch; my grandmother, Mama Loyes, was the last. After her death, while going through her things, I found a book called <u>The Magic of Believing</u>. It was a book about envisioning how you want your life to be and then believing in your personal power to make it so. Inside the book, in my grandmother's handwriting, was the inscription, "To my brother, George. This book is well worth your time, so *do* read it. Love, Loyes." Seeing that brought back a flood of memories about how much time my grandmother and her sisters spent trying to help George get his life together. He never did.

Worried that George would get drunk and freeze to death in that old house where he lived, the three of them clubbed together and bought him an electric blanket. Then, terrified that George would get drunk and crank his blanket up and set the house on fire, they huddled together and came up with a plan. Mama Loyes found a heated mattress pad at the department store where she worked that had tubing running all through it. Water in the tubes then heated up and the heated water kept you (or Uncle George) warm. This was the theory. Of course, their thinking was that if George got drunk and set himself ablaze, the tubes would melt and he would put himself out - all without ever having to wake up! I guess it never occurred to them that he might also electrocute himself but, jeepers, anything would be better than dying in a fire, you know?

My mother's brother was a mean drunk - a giant, gorilla of a man with a Marine Corps tattoo on his arm. He could slap the bottom of a new Ezra Brooks bourbon bottle so hard it would split the paper seal and send the cork ricocheting off the kitchen cabinets, a talent that sent everybody scurrying out of the house and away from him as fast as possible. My uncle could stay drunk and mean for most of the day.

Although he never missed a day of work because of it, my Daddy was a drunk for most of his adult years; actually, he was a terrified man masquerading as an alcoholic, but the effect was the same. He could be sloppy and obnoxious, or raging and hate-filled, and we never knew which Drunk Daddy was going to surface. This wrecked us as a family, but kept us on our toes - sometimes our tiptoes. Life changed for Daddy completely the night he got arrested for driving 12 miles an hour on the freeway on his way home from the lake and had to spend the night in what he called the "Gray Bar Hotel" in McKinney, Texas. To Daddy's enormous credit, he never drank another drop of alcohol after that. He said he wouldn't and, by golly, he didn't. To Mother's enormous credit, she didn't blast him with twenty years' worth of I-Told-You-So's, a monumentally difficult task for her. No doubt she developed a serious cramp in her tongue or knot in her throat for the rest of her days because of her restraint. I was as proud of how she handled herself just as I was proud of him.

Daddy, rising to the honor that forgiveness and redemption had just lain at his feet, became the great guy we were all surprised to learn was living in there. He was the most surprised of all, genuinely shocked at how much we all liked him and wanted to be around him, since, for most of our childhood and so many years later, we had all desperately scrambled to get away from him. Things change, I'm happy to say. And so do people - sometimes before it's too late to repair a life.

Daddy's father was a cattle rancher, widowed with two young sons to raise. He managed to snare a beautiful young schoolteacher as his new bride. Some months later she told him that she didn't think she could stay married to a man who never went to church. Well, he got drunk and rode his horse through the sanctuary at the next Wednesday night prayer meeting. I don't think he drank much after that and they did stay married for the rest of their lives, but I still don't believe he spent much of that time in church.

My Aunt Ruby, having been married for a time to a no-count drunk long enough to produce a son who staggered into his old man's footsteps, hated alcohol. Hated it. "I've just never seen alcohol do anybody any good," she would say, an understatement on her part. When her shiftless son (known to us all as "Billy C.") bought two liquor stores, Aunt Ruby was thrilled - overjoyed, even. Nobody in the family could figure out why. They speculated and they opined; they whispered and fueled the family buzz before somebody finally decided to be direct and ask her.

"Just why are you so dadgummed happy that Billy C. has purchased two liquor stores?"

"Well," Aunt Ruby replied, "he's ruined everything he's ever touched. I figure in pretty short order there'll be two more liquor stores out of business." And, of course, she was right. Her son didn't drink up his profits; they didn't get that far. Aunt Ruby's son drank up his inventory.

Some of us are born with what I call a Mainliner Personality, and I am one of those people. There is just no shut-off valve in me. This often creates havoc and disastrous results. Our family heritage is Scottish, Irish and Cherokee - see? We are screwed. I knew it.

Once, my cousin Herbie bought giant wine goblets that looked like they'd hold a quart or so and we drank our way through a couple of big bottles of some cheap sangria. I don't think we ever bought a bottle of wine that had a "bouquet". Shoot, ours didn't even have a cork. Our drinks of choice didn't even have what we called an aroma, either; it was more like an odor. Yeah, that was it. Odor. Anyway, deciding we needed even more of this stuff, and holding fast to our filled-to-the-brim goblets, we hopped into my shiny, almost new Ford Maverick for a quick run to the liquor store. We were laughing hysterically about something, I remember that part distinctly, when my goblet slipped from my grasp, bounced on the transmission hump, and sent the entire contents of my glass up into the air. The liquid, a big purple glob, quivered in the air for what seemed like a minute, taunting us, as if fate was actually giving us a chance to do something besides sit there and stare at it. Then, BOOSH! Sangria flooded my dash board and gushed deep into the bowels of my air conditioning ducts. The vents never moved again from their stuck position. And the inside of the car, from then on, smelled like happy hour at a bad bar, the kind of place where you'd have to buy beer in a long-neck bottle so you could break it and fight your way out.

You know how some things happen; how some moments change your life forever? This was one for me. No, I didn't quit drinking then, didn't even think about it. But I gave up on Sangria; and I sold the Maverick after a summertime road trip with my grandmother when running my air conditioner full-blast made her wake up with a hangover.

The dude who bought the car from me was Larry, a hippie-guy with grayish-green skin and chunks of candle wax in his hair. The reason for the candle wax was that he often got loaded and fell asleep on his couch until the candle burning on the end table beside his head melted into a puddle and molten wax oozed over onto his scalp. This was his alarm clock. Anyway, Larry lived in my apartment complex and sold dope out of his bedroom window, a drive-through for pot smokers. One day he stuck his head in my car, took a sniff and said, "Awwwright! This smells like my old Malibu!" And he bought the Maverick from me on the spot. He paid cash, of course.

If I could have smoked dope, I probably would have, but Larry never got a dime from me; no, I spent all my extra cash on alcohol, mostly cheap bourbon of some sort. Even later, when I worked for several years in rock 'n roll radio where there was plenty of marijuana to go around, I never smoked it. And it's not that I'm pure or prudish or even all that worried about breaking the law. I have allergies. And I'm a crybaby. Smoldering joints always smelled like somebody was barbecuing a Herculon couch. Dope smoke burned my eyes, made me gag, and clogged up my nose. I just couldn't do it.

Not only that, I carried around inside me the memory of my mother talking about this Hollywood person or that music performer, "...oh, he's just an old dope addict." As if that was the slimiest thing a person could become, right up there with being a Soviet spy or an atheist.

I remember watching a special on TV with her one night when I was in sixth grade about the making and trade of heroin. "But how do they make it?" I'd asked her. "What goes into it?"

"It's made from poppies, the flower," Mother had replied.

There was an alley my brother and I cut through when we walked home from elementary school. We were never supposed to go there. In the middle of one stretch of this alley grew the most beautiful, bright red flowers with black centers. The colors were so vivid it almost hurt my eyes to look at them. I asked my brother one day, "What kind of flowers are those?"

"Poppies," he said. Well. He might as well have yelled, "SNAKE!!" I whammed my body up against somebody's cyclone fence so hard I had diamond prints on the backs of my calves for days. From then on, whenever we scampered past those poppies, I strutted with my legs so high in the air I looked like a drum major being chased by a bobcat, lest a poppy petal glom onto my ankle and seal my fate as a heroin addict.

When I got older, it seemed far less torturous to get drunk. So, I got drunk, and with great regularity, usually with my cousin Herbie, but he wasn't the only one, and I wasn't all that picky. If you were sitting next to me and you were looking to tie one on, well then, you had somebody to drink with. If you were willing to risk your life with me for a little drunken fun, well, that was all the better. We'd be friends forever. I had the Wild Woman in me and while she was exciting and good for a thrilling time, she often took me right up to the edge of death. I once danced the Texas two-step around the outside ledge of a houseboat - the space was no wider than a saddle - on choppy, deep, unpredictable Lake Texoma. It was a cold, windy morning in March at a brunch where Bloody Marys got the best of most of us.

One time up in Gainesville, Texas, my friend Patti and her husband convinced me, after half a bottle of bourbon, that riding on a giant airplane inner tube tied to the back of their ski boat could be quite a bit of fun. All I had to do was lie face down on the thing and hold on. *Sure*, I thought, *that sounds easy.* Well. They didn't say how fast they were going to go speeding across the lake, nor did they tell me what would happen if they turned the boat sharply and I got thrown off, which they did and I did. Suddenly I became a human Frisbee rocketing thirty yards low and straight out, screaming through the air until I dropped and hit the lake's surface. Then I skimmed and bounced across a quarter-mile of water like a river rock - almost knocking myself unconscious. They came zooming up in the boat and picked my head up out of the water by my hair. I had a bloody nose and there was a buzzing feeling in my jaw, like something important was about to unravel or catch fire. Maybe both.

"Wow," Patti squealed, "what a ride! Wanna go again?"

"Nuh-uh, baby layda (maybe later)," was all I could manage to say, as my eye began to swell shut.

When I was drinking I felt so profound and privy to all the cosmic knowledge of the Universe. Great droplets of wisdom just waited to spill from my lips. Maybe I was just about to hurl. Granted, I often thought the other people around me were sloppy and boring. *Stupid bunch of drunken idiots,* I sometimes thought, especially when they were trying to out-profound me.

Some pals and I used to get tooted every Friday night sitting around the patio table beside my friend Shirley's pool. Invariably, the discussion focused on "truth" - what it is, what it's not, what we could do to stay hooked into that mode all the time. Shirley's position was that whatever is true for you, well, that's the truth. I said that we all look through a glass darkly, that our truth is colored by our experience, which may not match anybody else's. I do think, however, that there is a Universal Truth, a cosmic understanding of things and truth that we can all tap into from time to time - let's call it psychic energy, whatever. Actually, I'd have to get drunk again to recreate all the profundity that rolled forth from me that night and getting drunk holds no appeal for me at all. Now sober since 1988, I could try to give profundity another whirl around the dance floor and, still, I might miss the mark, so you'll just have to take my word for it.

Behind Judith, who was sitting across from me, was a large window in Shirley's den. Right beside the window was a lamp. The lamp was on a timer, causing the light to pop on each evening about eight pm. Judith listened intently to what I'd been saying, took a deep breath and replied, "I hear what you're saying, but you know...," she paused and leaned back in the chair with her index finger pointing upward. At the exact instant her finger popped skyward, the lamp in the den went *bink!* right behind her head, flooding her countenance with light, as if God had suddenly thumped Judith's noggin causing her to have the most brilliant thought of the century.

I looked to my right at Shirley and we both said, "This should be good."

My buddy, Sharla, is beautiful and petite, one of those women who look like they would never say anything obscene, not anything even close to doo-doo. You know the type. On our way to work one morning, we were heading to her daughter's Montessori school to drop off Dylan (age eleven or so). A guy in a red Jeep ran a stop sign and nearly hit us, so Sharla bopped the horn at him and he flipped us off. My mouth dropped open at his rudeness. "Did that guy just throw us the rod?" Sharla asked.

"Why, yes," I said, "I believe he did. How rude. I know, Sharla; catch up to him. I'll hang my big white butt out the window at him. That'll show him."

"I'll see your finger and raise you a moon!" she shouted.

From the back seat, Dylan asked, "You wouldn't really do that, would you?" I could hear her gauging the potential for embarrassment as we approached her school.

"Naw," I said, "not in this day and age."

"But in the sixties you'd have done it, right? Dylan asked.

"No," I said, "in the sixties I was still a good girl. But in the seventies I'd have done it." (And in a sizable chunk of the eighties, too, although I didn't mention that because I didn't want to downsize my cool quotient in the eyes of a kid who still thought I was pretty swell.)

You might wonder, then, since I'd seen so much pain and upset in my own family from alcohol abuse, why I continued to drink. I wonder that sometimes, as well, but I know the life of an alcohol abuser is often a big fat lie, one of denial and rationalization and, sadly, even justification. I could do all of those with the best of them. "Oh, I'm just under so much stress; I have to have a drink to relax." I remember saying that. The truth is, if I had waited for stress to completely leave my life, I never would have quit drinking.

All I can say is that people change for good when they are ready to. Never before. There is a picture of Daddy in my office on a bookshelf. He sits in a prairie rocker that had been in his ranching family forever, the exact same chair he and his twin brother had been rocked in as babies. In his arms he is holding tiny, newborn Johnny, my nephew, the only grandchild he lived long enough to see. It was Johnny's first day home from the hospital. It was also the first day in my life I ever heard my Daddy utter the word "precious." The look on his face is that of a man who had just fallen in love.

I keep the picture of Daddy where I can see it every day, not only because it is tender and dear, which it is. I keep it because when I see it, the kernel of sweetness in it is so bright, so dazzling - like gold - that it makes it easier to remember I forgave him. And it makes it easier to remember that Daddy became a man who allowed himself to be loved, the best gift he ever gave to us. Ever. I am not a brave or strong person, but sometimes I get lucky. By luck and only a tiny bit of willpower, one day I just gave the booze up. By luck, my drinking never got anyone hurt or killed. By the grace of God, I forgot what it felt like to have my mouth water at the thought of happy hour somewhere. I forgot what I thought was so wonderful about being drunk enough to tump over in the first place. Lucky me.

So now, when anyone says to me they've given up alcohol, I can look at them with understanding and compassion. I can see them though sober eyes no longer clouded by whiskey and smoke and regret. I can put my hand on their shoulder and give it a squeeze. "Good for you," I say, and smile at them. "You'll feel better and be happier," I tell them. Then I wiggle my glass of Diet Pepsi their way, like a toast. "And I'll drink to that."

"Forecast for tonight - dark." - *George Carlin*

Chapter 10 – The Nature of Things

Being a weenie in my family did not pay off - no way, no how. It was always better to learn to be brave right from the start. This was not always easy because little kids are often afraid and there are plenty of scary things in the state of Texas that'll put bravery to the test. The weather is one of them.

A Texas thunderstorm is an experience to write home about, if you live through it. For those of us who have never gone to war and don't intend to, this is as close to incoming artillery fire as we'll ever get. Texas clouds start hanging low and ominous, grayish-green and angry-looking. They crash into each other and when the sky really gets roiling and fuming, lightning splits the heavens open and thunder roars. Lightning once smacked the ground so close to our house I thought it blew the mailbox off the front porch.

When a Texas thunderstorm develops, smart people scramble off the golf courses, they jump out of swimming pools, duck their heads, throw down their aluminum softball bats and head for cover. If certain people are not so smart, then we stay right where we are and thumb our noses at Mother Nature, we keep on playing whatever games we were playing and doing whatever we were doing and hope for the best. Because, if the lightning weren't so scary, it would be downright beautiful.

Mother was determined that we would learn to appreciate the beauty of a Texas thunderstorm and she resolved we would learn to be in awe of the power of nature. Besides that, she was steady in her belief that she would not raise a brood of weenies. Now, don't get me wrong. She didn't let us play outside during a lightning storm or anything dumb like that. She didn't want us to be weenies, but she sure didn't want us to be fried weenies, either.

The neighborhood kids gave Mother the creeps when they scattered like turkeys as clouds rubbed together for more than a millisecond some eight thousand miles away and created a tiny rumble of thunder. Mother liked the other kids, but she was always appalled at their cowardly behavior. Something about their cowering was just so disgusting and just so, well, so chicken-shit, that it always seemed to me Mother was about to heave when she saw them skittering around the yard at the first drops of rain or screaming when lightning flashed across the sky.

Mother wanted us to be brave. She would calmly pull a couple of big quilts out of the top of the hall closet, gather us all with her on the porch, wrap the quilts around us and tell us stories about God's beard blowing in the breeze, and how a big clap of thunder was God sneezing or coughing as rain pelted the house and wind made the lid on the mailbox rattle, *banga-banga-banga*, right above our heads. Mother had an answer for everything, and God, bless His omnipresent heart, was the obvious culprit. It seemed to me that poor old God couldn't even have just a regular day without sending planet earth into a whirl-a-gig of natural disasters. We must have driven her crazy with our questions.

"What happens when God burps?"

"Typhoon," she'd answer.

"What happens when God blows his nose?"

"Avalanche."

"What happens when God stretches and yawns?"

"Earthquake."

"What happens when God toots?"

"Volcanoes erupt."

"What happens when God cuts his toenails?"

"Meteor shower."

"What happens when God whistles?"

"Tornado."

Zowie! Poor God! He must have been whistling the long version of <u>The Eyes of Texas Are Upon You</u> that April in 1957 when a tornado spent about half an hour tearing up a rather large portion of Oak Cliff, the section of Dallas in which we lived. Despite His splendor, I figured God must be feeling pretty rotten for having wrecked so many people's houses over something as simple as whistling, for heaven's sake. He needed to know we forgave Him so I proceeded to tell Him so night after night in my prayers for the next several months. "It's okay, Lord," I would whisper under the covers, "we all make mistakes. Now I know that you do, too. I think I even like you better now."

All Texans love a good story and Non-Texans everywhere say we exaggerate. We do, it's true, but never about the weather. We don't have to. Our weather is what it is, and often that is the worst Mother Nature has to offer.

Once, when Mother and Daddy were not home, a hailstorm hit, pelting our house with what sounded like rocks. Dean and I had left our bikes on the front walk so we scrambled outside to drag them up onto the porch. Then he dared me to ride my bike around the block in the storm. "If you do," he promised, "You can keep my lizard in your room for a week." Now, I wasn't all that wild about the lizard given that it didn't do much of anything at all, but a lizard was a cool thing to have, and I didn't have one. Besides, a dare was a dare, and it was a point of honor not to turn one down.

I bonged my bike back down the steps, shrinking my head as far down into my shirt collar as it could possibly go. On my bike I jumped and took off down the street. This was one of the dumbest things I have ever done, and as almost anyone can tell you, I have done some majorly dumb things in my life.

I did not pedal far on this day, maybe only down the street as far as the Coker's house. The hailstones were not large, more like the size of mothballs, but the sheer number of them was immense. This was like holding my head under a chute full of cascading marbles that ricocheted off my skull, knuckles, elbows and knees, blasting away at me with almost the force of buckshot. I kept my lips pulled tight so I wouldn't lose a tooth. Paying someone a dollar to beat me with a stick would've been easier.

Nuts to this big idea, I thought. *No lizard or dare, for that matter, was worth this kind of torture.* I screeched my bike to a halt on the gravel-like ice pellets and turned it around. Just as I did, a hailstone the size of a flashlight battery, a conglomerate of several frozen together hailstones, blasted straight from Mother Nature's slingshot and hit me square in the nose. Obviously, this was her best and last shot of the day. Fireworks sparked behind my eyes and the pain of it spiraled right up through the top of my head until I felt like I was growing a horn. I looked like the Cyclops in that movie where Kirk Douglas stabs him in the eye with the flaming torch.

"Aaaaaarrrgh! Aaaaaarrrgh!" I let out a muffled roar from behind my hand. The hail turned to rain as I staggerrd around like a punch-drunk prize fighter with blood streaming from my nose, cascading over my lip and pouring off my chin. I made my way back home only minutes before Mother and Daddy arrived and got my hair almost dried.

I looked like hell, though, like I'd been stung by a thousand bees and the blood had caked and dried around my left nostril. But my brother and I managed to convince our parents *(har-har-har)* that my bike had fallen over on me when I was putting it back up on the porch during the hailstorm. I'm not sure they bought it, but they never hassled me over it, which was a great relief.

Looking back I find it interesting to realize that even though I was a kid who fancied herself as a daredevil and someone as brave as a mean skunk with attitude, I was more happy to let my mother think I was some clumsy oaf who fell over a lot. I didn't want to worry her; I misled her so she wouldn't know all the truly dangerous and stupid things I was doing day after day to put my short little life on the line for some sort of glory. My brothers and my sister followed my line of reasoning. Of course, the flip side was probably that Mother was not really misled and was terrified we'd kill ourselves just stepping off the porch. *What will become of them?* She probably thought, *None of my children can even cross the street without breaking a collar bone.* No wonder she worried so much.

Texas weather definitely gave us plenty of opportunities to test our foolhardiness to the hilt. We forded swollen creeks, played football in the rain, rode our bicycles down an ice-encrusted hill just to see what it was like (it wasn't good), and waded through a storm sewer until we got stuck in the high water and had to pull ourselves up a concrete embankment by way of a skinny, rusty pipe. Although the pipe creaked and groaned and swayed, it managed to hang together long enough for us to make it to the top.

"They're gonna be fishing you kids out of the goddamned Trinity River," my Daddy said, as we sat there, shivering, wrapped in towels at our grandmother's house. And we knew he was probably closer to right than not. Garrison Keillor, who was raised in Minnesota, said he was from a place where, at least twice a year, nature tries to kill you. The same could be said about my home state, only the twice a year part sometimes came in six month stretches. We just never knew which six months it was going to be. The good thing about bad weather is, it kept us alert.

Life and the weather, however, were not always treacherous in Texas. Sometimes life was glorious and just so fine, the weather easy and lovely, and those memories I cling to as greedily as the ones where disaster was imminent. On warm summer nights in Texas when I was a kid the sky was so clear we could see the stardust. My Mom would spread the quilts out in the backyard and we'd lie on our backs, Mother and her pajama-clad crew staring up at the stars, making up stories about the moon. We'd ask a million questions.

"Why is it called the Milky Way?"

"What makes the stars?"

"Are there people in their back yards on the stars looking at us?"

And Mother would answer each question the best she could. When I asked her, "What is the moon?" she replied simply, "A reflection of the sun." In my little kid's mind, a reflection was an illusion, like a spot of light on the wall reflected off the mirror in Mother's compact, not a real thing or place to go. When President Kennedy announced one of our goals as a nation was to land a man on the moon, I thought, *Boy, are those guys gonna be surprised! They're gonna fly right through it!* I spent a large part of my sixth grade year wondering if I should call NASA and clue them in before they'd wasted all that money. My conservative Republican mother would have been so proud of me. I envisioned the headline,"*Eleven Year Old Worrywart Says Moon's An Illusion - Outerspace A Waste Of Taxpayer Dollars*".

There is a lot to know about the moon and I suppose that's why we went there so many times after we knew the way. For example, the moon revolves around our planet from east to west and is 238,857 miles away, as the rocket flies. This data and my experience with *Tang Breakfast Drink* are all I know about the space program, but it certainly is handy information in case Neil Armstrong ever challenges me to a game of *Trivial Pursuit*.

There are other definitions for "moon," however, that don't involve space travel, nor are they concerned with the hanging of a bare butt out the window of a moving vehicle. They have to do with how we feel in our hearts when we look up in the sky and see it shimmering at us, almost close enough to touch. These definitions are: "to spend in idle reverie," "to dream," or "to behave abstractedly," and these mean more to me when I think about the moon than any lunar crater measurement ever taken.

At least one night each month the moon gives us its very best shot, hanging low and golden in the open indigo sky. No longer is it 238,857 miles away, but right there, just...right...out...there...stunning us all, taking our breath away. We scramble into our homes, screaming to our loved ones, "Have you seen the moooooon?" Then we drag them out on the porch or across the driveway to Oooooh and Aaaaaaah with us and sit on the grass and admire the moon some more and maybe say thank you to God or the Universe or whatever power it was that thought the whole thing up in the first place.

The Native Americans call the moon Grandmother and that's always been a sweet thought to me - something beautiful and glowing, steady and dependable, something you can count on. Yeah, Grandmother Moon.

But it's more than that, you know. Lying in our back yard on a quilt, which always smelled vaguely like my Aunt Roxie, it occurred to me then (and I still believe it now) that my family certainly couldn't be the only family lying in its back yard admiring the moon. And if there was only this one moon for us all to enjoy, and we all did, then somehow we were all connected and not nearly as different as we tend to think. If the moon affects the tides and our moods and how rapidly our blood flows, then it is easy to understand how gazing up at it can make you kiss a stranger and fall in love. I find this thought most comforting - to know I'm not the only one who looks at a full moon, then wants to yell, "YAHOO!" and jump off the garage.

The moon is our touchstone, a luminescent reminder that we are all in this together. We sing songs about it, write poems about it and plant crops by it. We watch for it, stare at it and respect its power. So I have this idea, you see, one not too farfetched for a person with some time "to spend in idle reverie." As people across the world have taken a stand for freedom, demanding that their voices be heard, it is time for us to take a stand as well. Since we are trying to be pals with Russia, and if, at some point — praise God! — our nation finally figures out that invading other countries is a really bad idea, chances are we won't be needing that squillion dollar defense budget after all. So, with that in mind, whaddya say we cash in a big old bomber and put that money to better use? Yep, just drag that baby up to the recycling center and plunk it down. Then we can take that money and buy quilts for the world. Yeah, quilts would be good.

In the fall and winter we can all cover up. In the spring we can take them on picnics. And on those velvety, lukewarm summer nights when the deep sky is splashed with stardust and the moon glows in the darkness like a treasure, we can spread quilts out on the earth, our communal backyard. Then we can lie on our backs, gazing up at the cosmos, feeling at one with the world. And the moon. Thank you, Mother, for never letting up as you taught us the wonders of nature. And thank you, thank you, Grandmother Moon.

"He was not dumber than an ox; nor was he any smarter, either." - James Thurber

Chapter 11 – Lockjaw

Mother was a frustrated architect, I think, always drawing up plans so somebody could build something onto our house. We were a big family in a place too small, but I guess it never occurred to our parents to move because we never did. We just kept adding on...and on...and on. Over time, with constant rearranging by Mother and various contractors, our little post-World War II frame house was transformed from a two bedroom, one-bath home with a breezeway annexing a single-car garage into a five bedroom house with a den and a laundry room, an extra bathroom and no garage at all.

Before long, we began referring to our house as "the train," as Mother added boxcar after boxcar to our locomotive of a house. This transformation took place in two or three building frenzies, as I recall, where our house was torn to smithereens for what seemed like months at a time, a bombed-out shell of a home, and we lived with the dust and noise and mess. Each morning we awakened to the sound of saws and hammers and drills and clanking lumber and cement mixers whirring and sloshing. Dusty spackled men clomped through our house to complete some project or another day after day. We learned to live with the feel of grit mixed with Cheerios and milk each morning.

In some ways, it was also a dangerous time. We, our mother's accident-prone kids, were always stepping on nails or big staples or screws left behind and scattered around on the new, unfinished floor. We were a tennis shoe generation - and our sneakers were not like shoes of today with their soles as thick as cheesecakes. All that separated our feet from sharp and dangerous objects was a crew sock, a little luck, and a thin rubber-soled canvas tennis shoe.

During our second trip to the doctor's office on the same day (Dean stepped on a nail, we raced off to the doctor's office; then my brother Pat stepped on different nail as soon as we got home), Mother decided to just go ahead and get me stabbed with a tetanus shot. "Just in case," she told our doctor. He cackled like Dr. Mengele as he plunged the needle into my butt. Never once did Mother mention the word 'lockjaw' or just exactly why we were made to submit to this torture.

"What did I do?" I kept saying over and over, feeling totally double-crossed by this maneuver. "I could have stayed home, you know. I didn't have to come here."

"No, but now that you're here, you do have to get a shot," said Dr. Jackass. This took place during the first of our building frenzies. I was in the third grade.

A couple of years later, I'd gotten an entire rainbow of colored pens for my birthday and was pretty adept at tattooing any kid at my school who had a quarter to pay me. Broken hearts, Marine Corps emblems, anchors and American flags were my specialties. On this day, I was using the point of a big nail one of the carpenters had left behind on the counter to scratch an outline of the American flag onto my arm. Then I planned to color it in with my new pens. If I did it just right, the outline of the flag would stay there even after the ink washed off. This was my plan, a sure stroke of genius.

"Stop that!" Mother hissed at me as she snatched the nail out of my hand.

"Why?" I asked. "It doesn't hurt."

"I don't care if it hurts or not;" she said, "you're gonna give yourself lockjaw."

Lockjaw? I thought, *I've never heard of this disease before. Is it a new one? Did she just make it up on the spot like she so often does just to pound home two points with one swift blow of her motherly I-*

told-you-so hammer? I'd seen her do this before - more than a few times - cramming in every aphorism and moral of the story all at once and at every opportunity. When one of my brothers accidentally slammed the front door on his own heel and screeched with pain, Mother said, "See? That's what happens when you stay up too late on a school night." I fell out of the tree in the front yard and crunched my shoulder and Mother said, "Too many soda pops'll throw your balance off."

But lockjaw - wow - what a treacherous-sounding word! It is one that weighs heavy on a young kid's mind. I spent whole days just pondering the awfulness of it. Lockjaw sounded permanent, for sure, disfiguring and deadly, probably - right up there with polio, rabies, bubonic plague and radioactive anything.

"How do you get it?" I asked my mother.

"From doing stupid things like scratching on your arm with a nail," she said. "It's quite simple. Germs on the end of nails get in your bloodstream and you get lockjaw."

"What happens then?"

"Just what it sounds like, Jody. Your jaws lock."

"Open or closed?"

"What does it matter?" Mother said exasperated. "Either way, you'll be dead."

"But how?"

"You can't chew your food, you can't swallow, and you starve to death."

"Couldn't you chew my food up for me? Eskimo mothers do that for their babies."

"I'm not an Eskimo and you're not a baby. I'm trying to avoid the problem altogether, if you don't mind - and you've been reading too many National Geographics."

It was clear that if I was stupid enough to contract lockjaw, I would be on my own. No way was Mother going to chomp up my meal and stuff it down my gullet. "Got lockjaw, huh? Well, too bad for you," she'd say, "end of story. Bye-bye." In a way, I could even understand it.

This lockjaw was definitely scary stuff. Scarier, even, than my fear that my bad behavior would be etched on my Permanent Record, that dreaded report card in the sky, which would be sitting right there on God's desk, smudged, ragged, and loaded with addendum and paper-clipped notes when I showed up on Judgment Day. Boy, would I have some explaining to do.

God's voice would boom at me, splitting the clouds apart. *"SAYS HERE YOU DIDN'T LISTEN TO YOUR MOTHER... HMMMM... IS THAT TRUE? YOU DIDN'T LISTEN TO YOUR MOTHER WHEN SHE WARNED YOU AND PLEADED WITH YOU ABOUT SHARP OBJECTS AND GERMS AND RUNNING AROUND LIKE AN IDIOT?*

"HEAVEN IS NOT THE PLACE FOR FOOLS, LITTLE LADY, AND A PERMANENT RECORD LIKE THIS IS CERTAINLY NOT ANYTHING TO BRAG ABOUT. BUT I BET YOUR MOTHER, WHO IS PROBABLY THE SMARTEST PERSON IN THE WORLD, WARNED YOU ABOUT THAT, TOO, DIDN'T SHE?

WELL? DIDN'T SHE?"

Since God knows everything all the time, it would be pure foolishness to try to talk Him out of what He knew to be true. I, of course, would not be able to plead my case before Our Father Who Art In Heaven anyway because my jaws would be cranked open, probably, and permanently locked into the bear trap position. "Nnnnnnnnng! Nnnnnnnnng! " That's all I would be able to say, and I can't imagine that God, who would certainly be more than a little P.O.ed at me by this time, would want to hear any of my excuses, flimsy or not.

My brain would be screaming, *Wait! I was framed! Mother thought we were going to die all the time. She warned us about everything. Constantly. It was like crying 'wolf" - no - 'wolves!' - whole packs of wolves! That's how many different things she warned us about - all the time. How was I supposed to know for sure this was the one act of nitwit-hood that would do me in?*

It would be too late for that, though. My tokens would be all used up. God would place His omnipotent hand upon the heavenly lever marked 'EXODUS' and pull. *Foomp!* I would be sucked down a mother of pearly toilet shot through a gold-plated pneumatic tube and *Da-boosh!* There I'd be, doing the backstroke across hell's fiery lake for all eternity. This could be a problem. It would most definitely slow down my quest to be the only fifth grade girl at my school to hit a home run against the boys. Being dead would put me, as they say, out of the running, however, it just might make me a faster swimmer.

Even with the fear of eternal damnation and despite the fact that we were a pretty smart brood, overall, none of us kids in my family ever really learned our lesson,. My brother Dean got a dartboard for Christmas one year. It came with heavy-duty, brass, half-pound industrial darts. The "feathers" were hard plastic, that's how sturdy these things were. It was like throwing rocks with really sharp points. Finesse was not the name of this particular form of the game.

We were at our grandmother's house one Christmas day and had no place to put the board up to play. So, of course, rather than playing with something else or waiting until we got home to hang the dartboard, Dean, our cousin Herbie, and I stood on opposite sides of the street and sailed the darts back and forth at each other. We did not throw them hard and fast - no, no, that would have been dangerous. We reared back and threw them high, high, up into the sky so that they would make this lovely arc before screaming down like tiny missiles. The object of this game was to see how close we could nail a dart to each other without actually drawing blood.

Dean let fly a beauty. Herbie, normally an alert guy with quick reflexes, was standing on a brick platform by the porch. For some reason he froze just as the dart was headed straight for his head. He looked like a bunny rabbit in someone's headlights on a country road late at night.

"Duck!" I screamed as loud as I could and Herbie scrunched his head into his shirt collar and turned his whole body to the side. His head did not get stabbed. *Thwonk*! is the sound a metal dart makes as it pierces the sleeve of an oxford cloth shirt and enters a deltoid muscle. I can say it now and just save everyone the trouble of having to find that out on their own.

Dean flew across the street just as I eased the dart out of my cousin's arm. A dark red stain about the size of a dime slowly oozed its way onto the sleeve of Herbie's white shirt. I held my thumb on it to staunch the bleeding. The three of us looked at each other like the doomed children we were - *yipes*! What were we going to do? Just inside the door, not twenty feet away from us, was a whole house full of adults, all of them perfectly capable of snatching the three of us bald-headed for doing something as asinine as flinging metal darts at each other back and forth across the street.

The results of actually fessing up were ... grim. On the other hand, there was the dreaded lockjaw, which could render my cousin incapable of eating chocolate pie (his favorite) or anything else for the rest of his very short life. This was a dilemma. We huddled and discussed, then finally agreed to take our chances. Lockjaw, Herbie decided, would be easier to bear than the gaze of Aunt Jo (my Mother) when she was high-pissed, especially if it was because we'd all just done something really, really stupid. Also, we reasoned, Herbie had eaten such a giant mound of turkey and dressing only an hour before so that, even if his jaws did lock up on him, we'd still have plenty of time to speed him over to Methodist Hospital before he came anywhere close to dying. Certainly the people at the hospital would be able to save his young life.

Dean and I promised to keep an eye on him, which we did, for the rest of the afternoon and into the evening. When Herbie stretched and yawned after the football game, I lurched toward him certain this was the beginning of lockjaw. I watched his jaws move like Jerry Mahoney's for the rest of the day - through turkey sandwiches, deviled eggs, chocolate pie, cherry pie, German chocolate cake and brownies. Man, that kid could pack away the groceries!

By eight pm, I'd pretty much decided that a heart attack or an exploded abdomen were the only disasters that would befall my cousin any time soon. I could quit worrying. My brother who fretted very little over anything had quit watching Herbie for signs of imminent doom hours before.

Finally, as we were all getting ready to leave, Herbie's Mom, my Aunt Edna, spotted the bloodstain on Herbie's shirt. "What did you do to your arm?" she said.

Herbie and I looked at each other, our eyes frozen, our solemn collaboration sitting right there between us like the open door to a jail cell. "I, uh, I scratched it on some bushes outside," he said.

"Good thing it was the bushes and not something metal," Aunt Edna replied, "You wouldn't want to get lockjaw."

*"Any idiot can face a crisis. It's day to day living
that wears you out." - Anton Chekov*

Chapter 12 – Lost and Unfound

We lost Michael once at Galveston Beach when he was three
years old. The twins looked so much alike and moved so quickly it
often felt as if we were seeing two of them when, in fact, it was the
same twin running 'round and 'round. There wasn't a lot of things that
Mother and Daddy went absolutely bonkers about, but losing one of the
twins was one of those things. It was distressing to me to see Mother
racing around panic-stricken and flinging herself into the surf and
swimming out trying to spot a bright orange life jacket that somebody
might have missed. But watching Daddy panic, yelling out for Mike
while sprinting barefoot down the beach, was even more upsetting. It
was like witnessing all you have known as security coming apart at the
seams.

Mother sat down with Dean and me when the twins were first
born. She delegated each of us a tiny baby boy to look after. We were
three and four years old, respectively. Rather than having to keep an
eye on all four of us, she enlisted some help. "This is your baby," she
said to me. "And this one is yours," to Dean. "You are responsible for
him. Make sure he has a clean diaper, a bottle, a pacifier, whatever he
needs; and no matter what you do, make sure his life is never in danger.
If something goes wrong, yell for me or for Daddy."

The baby my Mother assigned to me was Michael. He would
forever more be "my baby". (Even now half a century later when I look
at Michael with a big portion of his scalp showing and his remaining
hair white, I still see him in a diaper and clunky high-top baby shoes -
it's unsettling.) This assignment was a big job for little children, a huge
responsibility and one that I took way too seriously. Really, all Mother
was attempting to do was to try to help Dean and I grow up. I
understand that. On that particular day at Galveston, however, after

having misplaced the child entrusted to my care, I felt I'd blown it and let everybody down; I'd lost my little brother at the beach and knew enough to know that Mother would never recover. After all, Pat and Mike were only three. I was six, and my skinny shoulders sagged under the burden of having just ruined my family.

Not for long, though. Within twenty minutes or so, twenty of the looooongest minutes of angst our family had endured up to that point, a lifeguard came walking toward us holding Michael by the hand. People on the beach around us began cheering, yelling for all the others who were scrambling around helping us to call off the search. Seems our boy, Mike, had been spotted about a half mile down the beach, strolling along, chattering away with various people who could not understand what he was saying any better than we could. He had been visiting. My shoulders perked back up. I stopped sobbing. Michael, my baby, had been lost, but, thank God, he didn't stay lost.

I've been thinking about that story lately and about how things suddenly disappear. It makes me crazy when things are right there and just moments later I can't find them. Granted, the things I misplace now aren't as important as my little brother and the loss of them won't wreck my family. Still, losing stuff makes me nuts. I don't think this is a matter of age, either, although some people might argue with that. When Uncle Charlie was ninety-two, he looked me in the eye and said, "Jody, I can remember what I did when I was nine years old, but I can't remember where I put the hammer yesterday." He leaned back in the rusty metal chair and dragged his feet in their white socks and sandals along the porch. His gaze went somewhere far, far past me and locked onto something from his boyhood.

"Want me to help you find it?" I asked, tugging him back to the present.

"What?" he asked.

"The hammer," I replied. "Want me to help you find the hammer?"

He thought for a moment then got that crinkly grin around his eyes, the one people get when they know you're about to realize they're smarter than they look.

"Naw, 'at's all right," he said. "If I find it, I'd just have to remember what I wanted it for and that might take longer than I have left. Better just let it be one of them things that stays lost."

Uncle Charlie was right - some things are better left lost. Other things would be better found, but they just stay lost anyway. I know, because I've been searching for them for years. During a bout of heavy thinking one afternoon, I realized I've spent approximately thirty minutes of almost each day I've been alive searching frantically for something. This is bothersome.

Mother once grounded me "...*for the rest of your life*" because I lost my Daddy's World War II good conduct medal while playing army with my brothers. A year or so later, I felt it against my cheek in the flowerbed after catching a football and crashing through the front hedge. Six months after that, I lost it for good.

My niece, Kelli, heard this story when she was a small girl. "So, Aunt Jody," "she said, "You lost Pawpaw's medal?"

"Yes," I said.

"And then you found it?"

"Yes."

"And then you lost it again?"

"Yes."

"Did you ever find it again?"

"No. No, I didn't."

"Oh, Aunt Jody, didn't you learn your lesson?"

"Well, honey, I was a hard-headed child and I'm trying to save you from a similar fate."

Little did I realize way back during my hard-headed childhood days that my penchant for losing things would become so time-consuming. Imagine my surprise when years later rather than searching for the meaning of life, I'd spend all my time looking for the books I'd bought that told me how to find it.

I believe in order, I do. I have special nooks and crannies and hooks and drawers for everything. The flaws in my system surface when the phone is ringing as I walk in the door, or I've really got to go to the bathroom, or I crammed something in my pocket when I went out to the garage, or I'm too lazy to get up off the couch and go put it away, or I didn't realize it was on top of my car when I drove off...and on and on. So, the saying at my house is, "There's a place for everything, but where the heck is it now?"

Here are the five things I lose most frequently:

Socks: Mother's cardboard box on top of the dryer was full of socks waiting for their mates, like prisoners on Conjugal Visit Day. Half of the missing mates never showed up. What a big surprise.

Glasses: Now that reading glasses are part of my life, I have a pair of them riding around on top of my head constantly. This makes it impossible to find them in my purse. And I've gotten so used to them riding atop my head, I forget they are there. By the same token, I doze off so frequently while reading that I now find it difficult to nap without the weight of my reading glasses across the bridge of my nose. This is starting to feel like some kind of disorder to me. Perhaps I should seek out a support group.

Earrings: I bet Vincent Van Gogh never had this problem.

Golf balls: I have lost enough bright orange golf balls to pave Pebble Beach.

Keys: My keys stay in my purse. Absolutely. Unless I go for a walk, then I put them in my pocket. Or, if I get something out of the trunk of my car, then I might leave them in the lock or...who knows?...I might leave them in the trunk itself. Or, if the load in the washing machine gets all lop-sided and I have to dash in and fix it before it knocks the wall out, then I might leave my keys on top of the box of laundry soap. Or, if I need something to pry the lid off a can of shoe polish, I might use my keys for that; then I might put them back in the box with all the shoe polish and put the box back up on the top shelf in the pantry and not remember it for days. Other than that, my keys stay in my purse. Absolutely.

There are other things, too, that vanish, and, even though I don't necessarily feel responsible for having lost them, still, I have to wonder, *Where do they go?*

For example, common sense, I lose mine at least once a day, particularly if I am exposed to power tools.

Muscle tone: This goes faster than you can say "Jack LaLanne." Nobody knows where, exactly, but "to the dogs" is a good guess.

Self-confidence: I last saw mine on a downhill ski run in Angel Fire, New Mexico. It was clinging desperately to a tree.

Computer information: People tell me they lose stuff in the computers all the time. I am terrified I'll never have another brilliant idea, so I write everything down in a notebook before I transfer it to a computer. Now three of my notebooks are missing. Shit.

Integrity and self-esteem: I am ashamed to say I lose these more often than I would like and whenever they go, they go together.

Tire tread: We do not leave this on the road. If that were true, by now we would have very thick, rubberized freeways that would never need resurfacing.

Equilibrium: The loss of this is especially devastating to anyone born under the sign of Libra. Also, it was pretty tough for the late high-wire artist, Karl Wallenda.

Youth: My youth was not lost. It was spent.

Virginity: And to think I guarded mine so ferociously for so many years!

Innocence: This has nothing to do with the loss of virginity. It has to do with shopping for groceries using your own first paycheck.

Teenage boys who walk away from their cars and leave the music playing so loudly it gives me a nosebleed: Where do they go?

Train of thought: Now what was I just saying?

Clearly, the answer to the question, "Where do things go?" is perfectly logical. The Bermuda Triangle is bigger than we thought. Whoever decided the Bermuda Triangle lies somewhere around latitude twenty-five to forty degrees north and longitude fifty-five to eighty-five degrees west was - how shall I say it - shortsighted.

Recent discoveries, made by me, show that the dreaded Bermuda Triangle is not just one little old piranha of a triangle, nosirreebob, but actually billions of triangles. In fact, a personalized Bermuda Triangle has been issued for every single person ever born. (And you thought I was bad at math...shame on you.)

Now, all of these individual Bermuda Triangles are encased in another gigantic Bermuda Triangle that undulates in a sort of hula-fashion to keep everything it has swallowed throughout time from sinking to the bottom and forming the dreaded Bermuda Parallelogram. It extends from wherever you were when you last remember seeing that particular earring to the not very tall grass by the fourteenth fairway to the space between your washer and dryer, give or take a few inches. And, since it moves around, this means that we are often at the effect of each other's Bermuda Triangle. *Oh boy.* Speaking personally, I know it is during these times that I could not find my butt with both hands.

This is clearly an important discovery, one that will surely make me famous, so I am happy to share it. My plan is to send a copy of this information to The Office Of The Legislator Of Undeveloped Discoveries (T.O.O.T.L.O.U.D.). Yes; I'll do that this week. I'll get right on it. Yes, I will. Just as soon as I find my book of postage stamps.

The Twins

*"Sometimes the strength of motherhood is
greater than natural laws."*
- Barbara Kingsolver

Chapter 13 – The Long Arm of The Ma

I grew up thinking my mother had the longest arms in the world, arms that could snake around corners to drag me back into the room when it was time to wrestle me into a dress for Sunday School; arms that could reach up into trees and pluck us all down, one by one, as if she were a mother chimpanzee whose baby chimps had all suddenly gone catatonic and didn't know what to do. Mother's arms could stretch down the entire length of a church pew to snap her fingers at my brothers and me for giggling and snorting and not paying attention to the Word of the Lord. Those arms of hers could extend all the way to the back of the station wagon to separate and smack whichever of us had gotten into a wrestling match back there. It was a startling thing to see, a wonder of some sort, certainly deserving of exhibition at the Texas State Fair. Or maybe even the world famous Smithsonian Institute would exhibit Mother's arms. From what I could understand, it was just like the Texas State Fair without the Fletcher's Corny Dogs and the bad smells.

When I look at pictures of her, Mother's arms don't look any different than anybody else's, but they were deceiving. When she needed them to, they extended like Gumby's arms, detaching completely from their sockets and stretching way, way, waaaaaaay out until she had the wing span of a heron, I swear she did, and on her face whenever her arms were doing that stretchy thing was the fierce, determined look of a mother condor. It seemed to happen most often when there was impending doom, but, gee, that wasn't hard for Mother to spot. Like a sworn enemy, impending doom was what my mother most watched out for.

I was six the day I learned to ride a bike, out in the front yard, on a blue hand-me-down Huffy Convertible bicycle my cousin Shirley had outgrown. I raced past Mother heading straight for the nandinas pedaling away as fast as my little legs would go. "Hit the brakes!" Mother screamed at me.

Brakes? I thought, *I only learned how to keep my balance ten minutes ago. How was I supposed to work so many different things at once?* Pedaling fast and hard was the only thing I knew how to do so far. Mother's arm stretched out and she snatched me up by my T-shirt, with my legs still whirling in the air, as my bike crashed through the hedge and up against the house, crunching an asbestos shingle like the shell of a hard boiled egg. "Rats," I said.

"You're gonna have to learn how to work the brakes, Jody, or you're gonna kill yourself." That was all Mother said as she dropped me onto the grass like a big sack of pinto beans. She was worried, though. After all, the combo plate of destruction and death, the full-meal deal of doom Mother could feel coming like a bad case of indigestion.

Mother paid attention to her dreams, too, especially those in which doom often showed its face and, apparently, she heeded everybody else's, too, because our entire vacation got re-routed over one. Uncle Bob awoke in a sweat one night, puffed his way through half a pack of Pall Malls, then called Mother and told her about his dream in which one of our twins had fallen into the Grand Canyon. This happened two days before we were to leave on our marathon three-week vacation. So, before she even went back to bed that night, Mother hunkered over the dining room table in her muumuu with a Tareyton smoldering in the ashtray, her AAA maps all spread out, and a Magic Marker squeaking away as she re-routed us around the Grand Canyon in Arizona and up through Mesa Verde National Park in Colorado.

Let me say right now that Mesa Verde National Park is beautiful, but no way is it canyon-free. It has plenty of canyons. Lots of canyons. It has steep cliffs with sheer faces, jagged rocks below, and plenty of ways to snuff any small child who managed to wander too close to the edge, something we were always doing.

At first, Mother didn't seem to notice the potential danger of us falling off or sliding down or crashing through something even though we stayed at a cabin there for several days. Or maybe, since the canyons at Mesa Verde were not as deep as the Grand Canyon, she found comfort in thinking our deaths would be easier to take if she could actually see our bodies and stand a chance of being able to drag them back up the mountainside, strap them to the top of the station wagon and take us back to Texas for burial. No place else but Texas would do.

Mother was more concerned about one of us being eaten by bears, and rightfully so. We had been warned about this danger but went looking for bears each day anyway as soon as we were out of sight of our parents.

This place, Mesa Verde, was just swell. Mother thought it grand that we were learning so much about nature and Pueblo Indian culture and that her children were getting to see places unlike any we'd ever seen before. There was a certain kind of serenity about her we didn't see all that often, as if she'd just passed another big Motherhood exam and only she could hear the cheers coming from angels in heaven. Not only that, the cabin we had rented was only seven bucks a night, a definite plus in her eyes. Lots of things could be overlooked if the price was right. Then my brother Pat almost fell over a cliff.

It was a bright day, very warm and we were on a walking tour with a bunch of other families and a park ranger, of course, who knew more about everything than anyone we had ever encountered in our young lives. All of it was true, too, or it certainly seemed to be. Not a single trace of pulling our legs (known in my tribal unit as bullshitting) was to be heard. I was very much impressed with this particular division of my federal government and began imagining myself as a park ranger in a crisply pressed uniform and a hat the size of a hubcap. I'd wow thousands of park visitors constantly with my wealth of knowledge, probably saving a life or two each year and getting awards which would decorate the walls of my cozy and comfortable log cabin. Plus, despite the dust, my shoes would somehow always manage to stay shiny and my pants and shirts would stay starched as stiff as poster boards.

Gazing out over yet another canyon, we were all oooohing and aaaaahing and God-blessing-America when I looked to my right and saw one of the twins gripping the underside of the guard rail which jutted out at a sixty degree angle over the abyss. It was my brother, Pat, with his little belly bowed out and the tippy-toes of his sneakers just barely clinging to the concrete. Pebbles of gravel and cement crunched and scattered and popped their way from beneath his feet and down the canyon wall. *Uh-oh. Doom again.*

I tugged at the bottom of my mother's blouse. She looked down at me with eyebrows arched over the tops of her cat-eye sunglasses in the 'What-is-it-look-of-impatience' she could get whenever we needed her attention but were supposed to be quiet. I pointed with my thumb toward Pat. Her throat always made this pneumatic tube kind of sound whenever danger was near, almost a snapping sound. Her noise alerted Daddy who lunged at the exact same moment Mother's arm did. Daddy caught Pat by the back of the pants while Mother's arm extended completely over my head, out of her arm socket approximately eight and a half feet, and caught her seven year old son by the back of his shirt. They both yanked so hard it nearly pulled poor Pat right out of his clothes. He could have easily been flung all the way back to Texas if they'd let him go at the same time. The Mesa Verde Incident may have been when Pat finally lost the rest of his baby teeth. They were probably jarred completely out of his little head. And odds are that his chronic neck problems stemmed from this time.

I always find myself wandering too close to the edge, but after Mother's death in 1986, I am not as cavalier as I was in my youth. This process called life has caused both my knees to go south on me and in the back of my mind is the fact that my mother is no longer around to snatch me back from Death's over-eager jaws. These two things are turning me into a wimpy chicken shit.

For example, in 1988 my friends Beth, Sheri and Linda and I moved from Dallas to Portland. On the way we stopped in Mesa Verde National Park to extend our adventures. Even now, the memory of that trip is so real, the story seems easiest to write by slipping into the present tense. I still feel the mountain breeze in my hair as we are sitting on a long wooden bench. One of us said, "The Native Americans who lived in Mesa Verde so long ago must have been bored."

"Otherwise," another of us said, "why in the world would they have spent that much time hacking villages into the sides of cliffs...:

"... and constructing unbelievably tall ladders to get from place to place?" another of us added enthusiastically.

I remember feeling witty and having fun. To the conversation I added, "Why didn't they just go hang out up on the mesa part of Mesa Verde - you know, up there where their corn was growing? That would have made sense."

That's when someone in my group said, "Let's check this out at close range on a tour." And everyone agreed, except me.

I'm a wimp, I think and cringe at my own cowardice. *Heights terrify me and I'm sure the fear is leaking out of my pores like sweat, and I am certain I smell musky and horrified like a ferret being chased, and that everyone sitting on this bench knows it's me. I am screwed, I know it.* But I do not say this out loud. Out loud I worry about my weird knees.

That's when our basic no-nonsense gal in shiny, sensible, government-issue Parks Service shoes arrives. Ranger Brickbat, our National Parks Service Representative, begins listing everything she can think of that might cause us all to be dead or at least a vegetable (her exact inspirational words) if we screw up and fall while on this little mountainside jaunt. My knees, never strong, have now become the consistency of aloe vera gel. Despite my admiration for her crisp uniform, I decide I don't like Ranger Brickbat a bit. "She is too dramatic," I whisper my complaint to my friends. "She's no fun," I whine. *She looks mean, that's what I really think.* All the time I'm trying to figure out a way to weasel out of this whole ill-advised, probably Satan-inspired, catastrophe headed our way. But whining never works for me and it doesn't again. There's no way out. No such luck.

Sometime during Ranger Brickbat's dire announcement, our trip leader shows up - Ranger Mom is bouncy with curly blonde hair and she looks like she wouldn't let you hurt yourself for a minute, nosirreebobtail. She has on jeans and sneakers. I feel better.

So, we skitter down the trail as Ranger Mom explains how the miraculous yucca plant can be used to make everything from loincloths - *Oooh* - to frying pans - *Aaah*. I'm having fun. Then we round a curve and I see it: Ladder Number One. *Oh God. Surely, that has to be taller than forty feet. Both Ranger Brickbat and Ranger Mom said it would be forty feet but that, that ladder right there, is taller than anything I have almost fallen off of in my entire life.*

I secretly try to figure out just how tall a forty foot ladder is. *If I stretched my own body out six and a half times among the yuccas and rocks and pine nuts and down the mountainside, would it look like that ladder? Or,* I fret, my worry taking another direction, *am I just having a premonition, a slow-motion look in my own mind's eye of myself scraping down the cliff?*

We stand in line, like sheep, waiting our turn. I shut my eyes trying to imagine what skin and muscle sound like as they peel away from the bone. All I hear instead is the imagined voice of Ranger Brickbat, heavy with disgust, as she points to my flattened torso some seven hundred feet below. *"See?"* she screams inside my imagination to the next group of tourists, *"That's what happens to stupid, wimpy chicken shits. That blob of flesh down there is a woman who thought she could make it up a forty foot ladder, but she was wrong. Do you hear me? I said she was wrong, wrong, wrong! Let me tell you something, people. Mesa Verde National Park is not the place to think you can do anything. You either do it or you die. Vegetable? Ha! She's a potato pancake if I ever saw one."*

Shaking the vision of Ranger Brickbat out of my head, I start up the ladder with my three pals. Sheri leads the way, then Linda, me, then Beth. My buddies Linda and Sheri are so sweet, so supportive, they say encouraging things to me like, "Hang in there, Jody" and "You can do it."

All the while Ranger Mom screams from up the top, "Don't look down!"

Suddenly, I hear Beth laughing hysterically just below me. I don't know why. We have paused for just a moment on the ladder and my legs have started shaking so badly that the ladder is now banging and bonging against the cliff. Beth can barely hold on. I am so embarrassed that I briefly consider jumping just to put us all out of my misery.

Ranger Mom yells again. "Go, go, go," she screams. "Don't look down, just go, go, go!"

So I go, go, go. Miraculously, I make it all the way to the top and push my back up against the wall of a cave. A small boy of seven or eight stops to look at me. In his big brown eyes I sense pity. That's okay. Pity I can handle; disgust is harder. I am thankful he is not Ranger Brickbat as we scamper on, heading for Ladder Number Two.

Heady with success, I suppose, I don't actually remember all that much about the second ladder or our scramble up the mountainside, other than the fact that we did make it. We seemed to be running at this point or maybe everything was just a blur for me. Maybe I'd already blacked out - who could tell? Certainly not I. At any rate, here we are, sprinting along, when we suddenly screech to a halt and hunker down to crawl through a skinny twelve foot tunnel. One of the other three thousand or so big fears I lug around with me at all times is my fear of teeny, enclosed places. But, of course, I have no choice here. If I want to get out, I have to go in.

I drop to my knees and begin scrambling through this tiny space when, suddenly, the Chapstick, car keys, sunglasses, and whatever other junk (flares, protractor, tire tool, several mechanical pencils, post-hole diggers, car battery, tire chains, duct tape and a length of rope, just like my Daddy) I have stashed in my left pants pocket gets snagged on a rock. It is not enough to stop this parade, but it is enough for the taste of doom and panic to sour in my throat. *I am screwed again, I know it.* Suddenly, with a flash of survival energy that seems to come from Heaven, I burst forward and explode like a newborn out the other side and into the sunlight. I feel as if my mother's strong, hyper-extended arms have yanked me to safety. Amazingly, I want to cry because I realize it was never the long arm of the law that kept me in check; it was the long arm of the Ma, the one that always came out of nowhere and snatched me back to safety, back beside her, no matter what. But Mother's not here now and I am a grown-up - what she always was. She cannot save me anymore; I must save myself. In this moment, I am so overwhelmed by Mother's absence, I think I'll sit right here on a great big rock and sob. It is a raw feeling, but rising up underneath the rawness is a small sense of exhilaration and empowerment. It's still in a distant way like a milestone middle-age birthday coming up, but I feel it.

Instead of sobbing on a rock, I beat on my chest and then punch my fists high into the air. I let out a yell like the winner Mother always wanted me to be, like the winner she knew I was, God bless her. I'll never be an explorer; never sail around the world in a washtub, nor jump out of a plane unless threatened with a gun or pushed. But today, and maybe only for today, I'm a brave girl. Victory is sweet.

"I sit astride life like a bad rider on a horse. I
only owe it to the horse's good nature that I am
not thrown off at this very moment."
- Ludwig Wittgenstein

Chapter 14 – Blizzard

Snow was rare where I grew up and, thus, revered. I remember Mother waking us late in the night to witness what always felt like a miracle. "I know you were asleep," she said, "but come and see, just come and see."

We gathered at the back bedroom window in our flannel pajamas, my brothers and I breathing warm, sleepy breath against the frosty pane as we watched the huge flakes, spotlighted by the yard light, float around in the sky and drift down to transform our backyard from the trampled-down, hard-pan, dog-shit-littered playground it was to a hushed place of wonder and beauty. Even the over-used and sad trampoline with its rusty steel frame and ripped canvas - the third one that year - looked almost pretty. Now a simple white mound in the yard, it looked like an igloo or a slumbering polar bear, as if its number wasn't up and its fate not already sealed toward a springtime encounter with Daddy's pipe-cutters. The snow was our friend, the silent homogenizer, covering up our messy life. The snow made us look respectable for just a little while before we ran outside to play in it, roll around in it, and scoop it up into snowballs to chunk at each other.

I am remembering of all this, believe it or not, as I slog across Wyoming in a snowstorm. It is early October in 1970, way too early for any kind of snow in Dallas, Texas but not, apparently, for Wyoming. The snow is coming down almost in sheets, like rain. *Is this a blizzard?* I wonder as I've never seen one before.

Interstate 80 is one icy rut after another. These ruts are made by big eighteen-wheelers with double trailers; massive behemoths that bear down on my back bumper and frighten me; gigantic, lumbering fortresses of chrome and diesel that spray my tiny, tinny-sounding Toyota with brown, frozen gravel and road oook as they roar past me. Clearly, these trucks and the tracks they make in the ice and snow are much wider than my little Corolla's teeny wheelbase. I've got one side of my car with wheels in a rut the other right in the middle of crusty, frozen slush.

My wipers are so ice-encrusted they begin clawing big scrapes into my windshield and I now know how a Pekingese dog feels or a Sheep Dog or just your basic, off-the-rack shaggy-faced mutt trying to see past all that hair in its eyes. But I'm afraid if I stop, I'll never be able to get going again, that I'll freeze to death (stuck to my windshield, probably) on the side of the road as the rest of the traffic rumbles past me.

This makes me wonder about the hitchhiker I saw earlier in the day - a balding young man oddly attired in a blue short-sleeved shirt and khaki pants, his thin longish David Crosby-looking hair whipping around his head in the gale of this approaching storm. His clothes, I remember, seemed so inappropriate for this weather, so unprepared and casual; he looked as if he might have just fallen out of plane bound for Florida. The young man squinted against the force of this winter wind as he held a flapping, hand-lettered, cardboard sign that said, simply, Yellowstone.

My car is cram-packed to the top with everything I own - so packed, in fact, the passenger seat in the front is overflowing with stuff falling onto the floor. Peering out the back window via the rear-view mirror involves craning my neck and shutting one eye. Otherwise, I would have picked the guy up and taken him at least to Laramie, which I know isn't Fort Lauderdale but it would have been civilization. *Boy*, I think, *Mother would have a fit over that one. I can hear her*, "What? A hitchhiker? Jody, do you want a one-way ticket to the morgue?" So, I keep the wipers on high-speed and make myself get used to that awful, fingernails-on-the-chalkboard squeak and the ragged, grinding sound of ice against glass.

I am driving back to Texas from Yelm, Washington, a farming community just south of Tacoma where I have been living for the past three months getting to know my biological father, my Bio-Dad, a man I met when I was seventeen. I am only twenty now, almost twenty-one, so our father/daughter relationship is a fledgling and tenuous one, but I'm glad I made the trip and the effort.

I've learned a lot. I've learned that I have another whole family of brothers and sisters I actually like; that our father, while probably not the best marriage material (he and their mother divorced, too,) is a handsome, smart, charming and funny man who is great for a good time and lots of laughs but who isn't worth twenty-five cents when it comes to personal responsibility. I've learned that charm is fun to see, but it doesn't pay the mortgage. I've learned that my stepfather, Daddy, with all his faults loved us all enough and took his role seriously enough to get up and go to work every day even when it felt like none of us wanted him around. I've learned that I miss my family and that I miss Texas. Besides, it's almost time for the Texas-OU game. So I'm heading home.

It would be safe to say that Dallas, Texas doesn't have a whole lot of snowplows. Okay, maybe one, but certainly not more than that. If we had snow - and it was never a sure thing - it came in January or February, was never more than four inches, and usually melted within a day or two. School was called off and we all played outside, making snowmen and throwing snowballs until our clothes were soaked and our ears and noses turned a dark almost scary shade of red. Once inside, we drank hot chocolate and took turns rotating all the socks and boots and jackets and gloves drying by the big gas stove in the den. Mother made ice cream from the remaining untarnished snow at the side of the house. We whispered to each other our hope that it would snow again so we'd have tomorrow be as much fun as today, but it was never to be in my hometown. The next day might be seventy degrees with the leftover snow melting as fast as cotton candy in a rainstorm. Needless to say, a snowplow was not something we ever saw much of in Dallas, Texas when I was a young kid.

But now, here I am on Interstate 80 in Wyoming in a blinding snowstorm. Wind and snow lash at my small car as I drive along. I am young, but no longer a kid. I am trying to get home, just like all of us driving in the slow lane are probably trying to get someplace important, but it makes, driving so very slow and that seems ridiculous and my patience with this pace is wearing thin. *I could grow a tooth or go through menopause before I get back to Texas if we keep driving this speed*, I think restively. I am a Type-A personality trapped in a Type-B body, in a Type-C car, in a Type-D traffic jam. *I might break out in a rash.* My fingers twitch from impatience coiling inside me like a spring. *I can't stand this.*

Suddenly, feeling bullet-proof, I yank my steering wheel to the left, slide over into the fast lane - buzzzzzzzzzz around a little in the slush until my tires gather purchase - and before you can say, "Young girl, small car - bad combo", I am racing past them all. I am whizzing past every truck, every car, every person I think is so stupid and so slow and so, well, just so chicken-shit they can't bring themselves to work up to half of the speed limit on this frozen freeway. There's nobody in front of me in this fast lane! I zoom and zoom and zoom! I pass them all, HA, HA HA! In the slow lane, in the very front of this very looooonnnnng line of cars and trucks is the culprit - the reason why everybody is creeping along like Houston Oiler defensive linemen on a hot day - the snowplow. So what do I do? Of course, it goes without saying, I do the most asinine thing imaginable - I pass him, too!

It is a blunder. When I am very old and on my way out of this life, someone will ask me," Jody, any regrets?"

I'll know then, as my time here draws to a close, that I should probably say, "Oh, I could have been kinder" or "Oh, I wish I'd been more considerate" or, even, "I regret not having written another book." What probably say, however, is, "Man, I should never have passed that snowplow!"

The snow and ice is getting meaner by the second. It looks like dusk although I can't imagine it being that late in the day. It feels colder, too, as darkness begins to creep across the mountains like a giant, gray cloak. Now, having passed every vehicle there is to pass, I whip back over into the slow lane and zip along. Way up ahead of me I see one truck. It's big and lonely and I'm sure I can certainly overtake it as we head into a curve. I ease back over into the fast lane to do this as ice crunches and scrapes beneath my car threatening to tear out the floorboard.

I've made another blunder because the ice and snow are considerably deeper and much harder in the fast lane now. My wheels feel locked in place - I can't turn them - and then I start to slide. It's a fast, hard slide to the right as my wheels slam into the crusty hill of ice built up at the side of the rut. This spins my car around. I take my hands off the wheel and my foot off the brake because I can't tell which way I'm spinning or going. I hear the blast of the trucker's horn and hear him hit his air brakes. My tiny, tinny-sounding car whirls 'round and 'round across the freeway in front of the eighteen-wheeler then I head backwards off the road. *Mother was right - Dead in a Ditch, here I come.*

I'm flying down, down, down a big hill and facing the wrong way. *Is this the hour of my death, the end of my life? Oh, Lordy, Lordy, Mother will be so upset...* and here come those thoughts, just like I knew they would: *IshouldabeenkinderIshoudabeenmoreconsiderate Ishouldneverhavepassedthesnowplow!*

Suddenly everything stops. Everything is hushed. My breathing and the banging sound of my heart is all I hear. I wonder if I am dead because I don't feel hurt; I don't see any blood. The snow begins to cover my windshield. I pull on the door handle and push against the door with my shoulder until I realize *I can't get out of my car. The snow is too deep.*

In that instant, as if yanked by God's own hand, my car door whooshes open. God grabs me by the jacket, drags me out of the car, and begins shaking me back and forth. My feet dangle like a puppet's. *But wait! God wouldn't be this mad, would He? I know I've already done a lot of bad stuff in my young life but, jeepers, you'd think He'd be a little happier to see me. God wouldn't be taking His very own name in vain, would He? I mean, God is really, REALLY pissed.*

God shakes me by the shoulders and yells, "Goddammit, who do you think you are? Jesus Christ - what the hell were you thinking - you could've gotten us both killed!"

I cry and blubber, feel the snot start to freeze on my upper lip as God screeches at me and shakes me around in the snow until I hear a man's deep voice yell, "Let her go!" It must be God's Grandpa, because God suddenly flicks His hands and drops me like a hot rock. I crumple onto the snow like last week's birthday balloon.

It is then I realize what's happening. I am NOT dead. God has NOT been slinging me around the snow. The man who's mad enough to throttle me is the trucker I tried to pass before I spun 'round and 'round in front of him. He's the very same trucker who jammed on his brakes to keep from slamming into me and whose eighteen-wheeler is now jack-knifed across the freeway blocking all of Interstate 80. *Oh boy.* And my hero is not God's Grandpa at all, but another trucker who has bounded down the snowy hill not only to keep me from being killed, but to tell the other driver he's got a chain long enough to attach and they can pop the cab around to get the other guy's rig straightened out. I stagger to my feet in snow up above my knees, fall down, get back up, and do it twice more before I can stand upright. I feel punch-drunk, although nobody has ever actually slugged me. I have to fight off the urge to say, "Do I look familiar to any of y'all?" But I'm still alive. There's hope.

Then there are more heroes, more hope. Two old farmers crawl out of a battered Ford truck and amble down the hill. In the back of their pickup is a rag-tag group of only-partially-frozen hippie hitchhikers sharing one thin, dirty blanket. They instantly begin tumbling out of the truck, too, and head down the embankment toward me. "Need some hep?" The old man in the flannel shirt shouts out to me. He's got a toothpick in his mouth. His jacket is open and flaps in the wind. His jeans are grimy and I can see bright, royal blue suspenders holding them up, even though he's got quite a paunch.

"Yessir, I sure do."

"These boys'll push your car back up on the highway. It'll hep warm 'em up."

The hitchhikers surround my car like a swarm of worker bees, slip it into neutral, and shove it forty yards up the snowy hill. People now stuck on the freeway - people I passed just moments ago, people who, by all rights, should be enraged at me - get out of their cars and cheer. Other folks honk their horns and flick their lights. The hippies bow and wave like Olympic champions. Truckers, now with their rigs lined up properly on the highway, gear down and take off at a crawl, blasting their air horns. I feel forgiven, somehow; unworthy of it, but forgiven, nonetheless. The two old men take me aside.

"Young people always want to get places too fast," the one with the suspenders says.

"They surely do," his compadre agrees.

My hero in suspenders continues, "I told him a while ago when you passed us, I said, 'That girl's gonna wind up in a ditch if she don't get her foot out of it' - and, by damn, if you didn't."

"You surely did," his buddy says.

"Now, we ain't here to tell you how to live your life, young lady."

"No, no," his friend firmly agrees, "We wouldn't want to be doin' that."

"They's a time for goin' fast, and they's a time for goin' slow."

"Yes, indeedy," says his pal, "there surely is."

"And if you want to live long enough to go fast again, then make sure you go slow enough today, 'cause this is a slow day. Get me? This is a slow, slow day. Fast'll get you killed on a day like today.

'cause today is a slow day. Drive fast on another day when the sky is blue and the road is dry. But not on this day, 'cause today is a slow day. Yes, ma'am, it's a slow, slow day." Hero-buddy takes the gnawed toothpick out of his mouth and tosses it into the snow where it lands like a mini-javelin. Then he turns and looks me right in the eye. "Are we clear?" he asks me. His friend, who is taller, leans his face in and down toward me to help make sure I get their point.

"Yessir," I say, "We are very clear." I realize this is the kindest and most gentle ass-kicking I may ever receive in my whole life as we trudge back up the hill.

I hug the farmers' necks, wave to the shivering hitchhikers in the back of their truck, hop into my tiny, tinny-sounding Toyota and slither my way back onto the ice-covered, creepy-crawly lane of Interstate 80 in Wyoming. The wind has died down some but the snow keeps falling. Huge flakes spotlighted by our headlights drift down pure and clean and magical, covering up the evidence of my blunders, covering up my impatience, covering up my messy life.

Being in this slow lane now calms my spirit and releases my shoulders. It allows me to breathe deeply and whisper, "Thank you. Thank you to the truckers, to the farmers, to the hippie hitchhikers, to all the other drivers. Thank you to my Mother who taught me that snow is wondrous and beautiful. Thank you, even, for this gift of my messy life."

I feel grateful to be alive; grateful for the acts of forgiveness; grateful to some force bigger than I can even fathom. And that's where I stay on this slow, slow day, cradled in the lap of forgiveness. And wonder. And beauty. All the way to Laramie.

"Generosity lies less in giving much than in giving at the right moment." - Author Unknown

Chapter 15 – Laramie

Dusk and I arrive in Laramie at the same time - just in time - to keep me from being stuck in the blackness of night on the frozen freeway, heading in a wrong direction towards Casper or Juneau or the Yukon or someplace in the tundra where I, as a Texas girl who's never trudged through snow deeper than her shoelaces, have no business going. Unable to tell the difference between a curb and a curb cut in a driveway, I accidentally get my tiny tinny-sounding Toyota stuck in the snow and ice on a curb and can't move it off. I buzz the wheels until they smoke; get out and rock the car back and forth until the knees of my jeans are soaked from slipping down onto the ice behind it. The wind and snow whip around me.

The streets all look deserted from where I am. Clearly, most people in this town have the good sense to already be in and hunkered down for the night. I crane my neck to peer down the road. There, headlights come my way. In desperation, I scramble out onto the icy street and flag down this sole passerby for help. The driver, a youngish bearded Paul Bunyon-looking guy, unfolds his big self from his Jeep and ambles over to the survey the mess I've gotten myself into. Snow, wind, ice, and the possibility of impending doom don't seem to be a big concern of his. Wearing jeans, hiking boots, a flannel shirt and down vest, he looks as calm and at ease as he might look on a summer day at the park. Compared to me, since I am now shaking so hard from the cold and terror that I seem to be stricken with some sort of palsy, this guy appears to be on Valium or something. I feel calmer just standing next to him; not what you'd call "peaceful," mind you, just not so jittery that I'm about to wet my pants. Or throw up. You get the picture.

He is a huge man, six and a half feet of muscle with dark, curly hair, a big beard, and a good heart (as I am soon to learn). "Do you think you can get your Jeep up here and push my car back off into the street?" I shout to him over the wind.

He shuts one eye and seems to be thinking about it, then shakes his head no, somehow conveying the impression that my question is a really poor and stupid idea - but I must say, he is nice about it. At least he doesn't hoot like an ape or instantly fall into a wheezy *har-har-har* like a jackal. "That might really mess up your front end," he says. I glance down at my grimy and mud-spattered coat, sweater, and pants, wondering just how much more messed up my front end can be, when I realize he is speaking of the grillwork and the hood of my car. He walks around my frosty and filthy Corolla, looking at it as if it's a Tonka Toy with a mind of its own that had gotten loose from the toy box and made its way to Wyoming. He whaps his bear's paw of a hand flat against the door panel and we both hear the bong of thin, crummy metal, but the fact that the car didn't just flop over on its side rather pleases him. It seems to almost startle him, actually. Toyotas are fairly new to America at this time, and, apparently, mostly unheard of in the Grand Tetons, where people get around in GM or Ford vehicles or, if they're a more serious mountaineer, a Jeep or International Harvester. He stares at my Corolla some more, shaking his head. "What kind of car is this?" he shouts to me over the wind.

"Toyota!" I scream back, as the gale flaps my jacket open-close-open-close-open.

"Huh," he mutters, "Jap."

Sometimes in your life things happen that you know you will never witness again - and it does, the miracle happens. And I haven't ever witnessed anything like it since. This miracle has nothing to do with God or angels or parting seas. Not even rainbows or Charlton Heston's voice blasting through the clouds. It's a miracle of brawn and of good heart. This huge man bends down and grabs my dinky little car by the front bumper, hoists the whole thing up to just about his waist, pivots, then drops it back onto the street where it lands with a crashing thud. Under normal circumstances, this would probably have blown my tires out. However, since the tires are frozen, each of them packed solid like forty pounds of ground chuck, the whole jolting maneuver serves to knock all the crusty ice off my wheels. *Woo-hoo! I am free to go again!* Then the big guy is back in his Jeep and motoring on before I even have a chance to hug his neck. All I can do is stand in the icy ruts on the street and wave as he drives off.

I bounce around Laramie like a pinball from motel to motel. Each one is completely full and there is no room at the inn - any inn - for me. *Jesus, Joseph and Mary, I understand your plight more than ever before...and on a donkey, too! I'm sorry if I never gave you enough credit for what you went through...* After an hour or so of driving, and after being turned away from every motel in Laramie, I find a phone booth close by the last one and call my mother collect. "Mother," I tell her, "my voice is shaking because I'm cold, not because I'm scared." Of course, this is only partially true, but she doesn't need to know that. "There are no motel rooms left in Laramie tonight," I continue, "and we're right in the middle of a blizzard, I think, so I'm going to cover up with my coat and sleep in my car."

Even over the blizzard's howling wind, even through almost two thousand miles of phone lines, I can hear my mother's throat make that snapping, pneumatic-tube kind of sound it always makes whenever one of her children is about to bite the dust and she knows it. Mother erupts. "Whaaaatt?" she screeches brutally loud and fierce. "Are you insane, Jody? You'll wake up in the morning as frozen as a bag of Popsicles and dead as a doornail! You march right back into that motel and tell them your mother said to let you sleep on the floor or I'll be driving to Wyoming and they'll have to deal with me. Go on, go do that right now and then call me back." She hangs up.

Crap. I hate it when she does this - makes me threaten somebody else with the wrath of my mother. I mean, they'd understand if they knew her, honest to God, they would, but... Crap. I hate it when she does this.

I trudge back inside the motel and try to look as pitiful as I possibly can. Luckily, this is not difficult since, clearly, I am in a pickle, a big, frozen pickle. I've been driving in a blizzard all day, have

spun off the freeway backwards, been slung around in the snow by a
trucker mad enough to kill me, got my car jacked up on a curb and
stuck there until I was rescued by a lumberjack super-hero. I am
muddy, sweaty, salty, crusty and I have the musky and terrified smell
of some odd little nicotine-addicted rodent who's been chased all day
by wolverines before dying of heart failure at the dump. I can't imagine
looking or smelling much more pitiful than I already do. Now my
mother wants me to threaten the only people alive in this town who
might help me, probably the only ones to notice my frozen corpse in
the little blue Toyota in their parking lot the next morning.

Crap... I hate it when she does this... But it reminds me that I
should write down my mother's phone number and pin it to my jacket
so they'll know who to call.

The lady behind the counter is nice enough, but no help. She
and I are alone in the lobby. I don't know what else to do except just
tell her. "My mother says," I begin, but the woman holds up her hand
and cuts me off.

"I know," she says, "your Mother thinks you should be able to
sleep on the floor right here in our lobby or on that saggy couch over
there, but I'm telling you that you can't. It's against the law."

"There's a law about this?"

Yep."

"Even during a blizzard?"

"Yep."

"Who thought up this law?"

"My boss."

"So, you'd lose your job?"

"Bingo."

"My mother might drive up here, you know. It wouldn't be pretty - sort of like letting a bobcat out of suitcase...and you know how the bobcat would be just a little more pissed off when you let him out than he was when you stuffed him in there."

"That's a chance we'll have to take. Besides, it would be my boss's problem then, not mine."

"So, you think it'll be okay if I just sleep in my car in your parking lot?"

"Oh, God, don't do that - you'll freeze to death! It's supposed to get down to twelve below or something." She eyeballs me funny, like I might be a Communist or something.

"You're not from around here, are you?" she asks.

"Of course, I'm not from around here. I'm from Texas. If I were from around here, I'd be home someplace in front of a fire! I wouldn't be standing in a motel lobby begging for shelter..." Suddenly, all of it - the whole stupid day - is just too much. I am overwhelmed. My voice trails off and I feel myself begin to whine, only it turns on me and comes out as a yelp, then a howl, and then, before I know what's hit me, I am sobbing and slobbering and banging my hand on their counter with my head tucked in tight against the crook of my elbow. I wail for what seems like several minutes, and then I stop, gasping for air between puny little hiccups. *Life (hic) is (hic) hopeless (hic, hic, hic).*

After a few seconds, the lady pokes me on the shoulder in slow motion with a pencil, like how she would poke something to see if it's still alive but from a safe distance in case whatever it is she is poking is playing possum (secretly alive and deciding on just the right moment bite her fingers off). In this case, she'd be right. I stop sobbing and hiccupping but I don't look up.

"Fwat?" I snarl at her, my face still against my arm. Crankiness quickly replaces hopelessness and makes my blood start to chum. I've had a terrible day. It feels good to let her know I am mad at her. *Jackass.*

"I'm going to tell you a secret," she says, conspiratorially.

"Grade," I mumble, annoyed, "ahm fure dadd'll pert be rye dup." (Great. I'm sure that'll perk me right up.) My nose is severely clogged. I keep my head down but I move my arm away from my face so I can see. And breathe. Snot and tears glisten on the counter in front of my eyes. The lady leans in by my ear.

"I heard they are renting rooms at the college for ten bucks."

My head juts straight up like a Jack-In-The-Box. The lady hops back. "Are you sure?" I ask. I feel desperate and hopeful all at the same time - *how can this be?*

"That's what I heard," she says.

"Where's the college?" I ask, swiping my sleeve across their counter to erase evidence of my meltdown.

"Two blocks that way," she says, pointing, "then turn left and it's right there in front of you. I mean, you can't miss it, for Pete's sake - it's a University, and it's big! Just find a place to park. Trust me - nobody cares where you park when there's a blizzard, just try to stay on the street and don't park in somebody's yard. Do you have ten bucks? I could loan it to you..." I guess I must have looked even worse than I thought, like a bum or a beggar or something.

"No," I say, "thank you. I have ten dollars." I pull a crumpled wad of ones and fives out of my pocket. "See? I have it right here, see?" I hold the bills up in front of me.

The lady raises her fists up beside her head and yells, "Yaaay! You'd better get going, then."

I scramble around, gathering all my stuff and pulling myself together. "Thank you," I say, again and again, "thankyouthankyouthankyou," as I race out into the freezing night. And she's right. It *is* a University, and it *is* big, and I *don't* miss it, and they *are* renting rooms for ten dollars - except, by the time I make it up to the counter, the last room has been rented by the elderly couple that burrowed into line in front of me. I mean, they didn't even say "Excuse us, please," they just angled in like God had given them special privileges because they had a pension and an Oldsmobile. *Jackasses.* But I am too tired to wiggle or argue at this point. I am too tired to even cry. I'd let myself get even more furious about this if I thought it'd do any good. But I don't. Besides, I've already thrown one majorly honkin' fit today and I don't think I can even muster another. *This is how cattle must feel on the way to the slaughterhouse - just finally they give it up, stare straight ahead, and don't worry about whatever's going to get 'em.* I look at the young girl behind the counter. "Okay if I sleep in a chair in the lobby?" I ask her. *I'll just sit there and pout and stew in it for a while. That'll show 'ern.*

"Sure," she says, smiling. "Want some magazines to read?" She hands them to me, still smiling, and automatically I smile back. A kindness - it registers. I feel better. The clawing scowl on my face starts to let go.

So, I snare a big, comfy chair, thumb through the magazines, get bored with that, rummage through my bag and find my U.S. road map. I am staring at this map when another young girl comes and sits across from me. She fiddles with her hair, checks her watch, waiting for her boyfriend to show up so they can go get ice cream.

"Ice cream?" I ask, incredulously.

"We're from Wyoming," she replies, which, I guess, explains it.

We chat some more. When I tell her about my day, about all the events of this very loooooooong day and all the things that led to my being in this big overstuffed chair right here and right now, she gets a big idea. "Hey," she says, "You don't have to try to sleep upright. I have a sleeping bag - you can sleep on the floor in my room!"

So, we trudge upstairs. Turns out another girl knows about an empty bed a couple of doors down. The girls on this floor of the dorm, suddenly and collectively decide it's their duty to take care of me. We get me settled in. I take a shower and get cleaned up. Washing off the grime of this day feels good. A clean sweater and fresh jeans help, too. We all traipse out into the blizzard to a cute place they all know that never closes - no matter what - and we eat hot dogs together. Snow and wind don't seem to bother anybody in this crowd. We drink hot chocolate. We laugh and laugh. They all want to hear the story of the icy freeway, the truckers and the hippie hitchhikers over and over. More people come in. Everybody seems to know everybody else in Laramie. Now the new folks want to hear the story, too. I tell it again and again. It gets funnier each time! They think I am so swell and I don't remember ever being quite so clever or popular in my whole life. How come nobody ever told me about Wyoming? What a great place! I might have to move here.

Finally, we all bundle up and head back. On the front lawn of the dorm a snowball fight breaks out. I get clobbered, but I don't care. I laugh and laugh when, suddenly, the laughter clogs in my throat like I've just been strangled. *Mother! Oh, Christamighty, I forgot to call mother back! She's probably already got the Highway Patrol out looking for me. They are crawling all over Wyoming by now, looking for me, and I'm whooping it up in a snowball fight - crap! Broderick Crawford's gonna come peeling into the parking lot at any second and kick my ass. I'll hear him yammering to my mother on his Police radio as I sit handcuffed in the back seat of his patrol car.*

"Yes, Mrs. Seay," he'll report to her over his radio; *"we found her. Yes, ma'am, I kicked her ass, yes, ma'am, just like you said. Well, you're welcome. 10-4 to you, too."* I race inside, find a phone, and call my mother collect. She sounds sleepy but calm. This surprises me. My brain fidgets for a proper story to tell her - I'm afraid I'll say too much.

I hem and haw a bit and realize I'm going to short-circuit just from the pressure of it all. So I tell her the truth - all of it, or almost all of it - about the lumberjack hero who picked up my car, about the lady at the motel, the girls at the college, the hot dogs, the snowball fight, the friends I've made. She laughs and laughs. Once I'm home, I'll tell her about the icy freeway, the truck drivers and the hippie hitchhikers, but for right now I want her to know I'm safe. I want her to know I'm being cared for and looked after by people who didn't have to but they did, in this snow-covered town called Laramie.

"So, you weren't worried?" I ask.

"Well," she says, "I won't say I wasn't worried. I fretted for a while. Then I realized there was nothing I could do about it. So I prayed for a little bit. That's when I concluded that you were either dead in a ditch - or - you were busy telling stories about almost being dead in a ditch. I was just thinking of calling the Highway Patrol when I fell asleep."

"Love you, Mother."

"I love you, too. Come on home. Be safe."

And I did. And I was.

*"If you think nobody cares if you're alive, try
missing a couple of car payments." - Flip Wilson*

Chapter 16 – Slick

Logic should have told us that Mother's fear of our winding up dead in a ditch might subside as we headed into our young adult years - ordinarily - but, alas, we were not a logical group, nor did we get much smarter as we got a little older. We were after all, Mother's children, just as she raised us to be; only now we had cars. Mother's children plus cars - not a very good combination. *Big trouble.* Ditches seemed more inevitable than ever. I'm sure Mother and Daddy both knew it was only a matter of time; in our case, time after time after time after time after time.

On a hot day in Dallas, Texas after a sudden summer rain and following a long stretch of dry parching weather, the Stemmons Freeway assumes the characteristics of a banana peel. It's the combination of oil, tire residue, heat, water, and whatever else the concrete has to offer that creates a film just slicker than duck shit. It can send cars careening every which way faster than you can say, "multiple-car-pile-up." I've seen it happen up close and personal.

Let me take you back to that day that I was slippin' and a-slidin', even peepin' and a-hidin' along this big thoroughfare before I very nearly became the meat in the middle of an squashed automobile sandwich. Watch your footing. Hold onto me, if you need to. Like I said, it's slick.

It is the summer of 1971. August, I think, a Saturday. I have promised my parents I'll meet them and some aunts and uncles at our cabin up at Lake Texoma a couple of hours north of Dallas, but only after I've run several errands. I am on Stemmons Freeway, driving too fast in a car too small after a sudden rain, but my tires are good and I am young, so I'm feeling bullet-proof, of course, like most young people feel behind the wheel of a car; not all that different, actually, from how I feel when I've had my oil changed. I don't know why these two things affect me the same way.

I am rounding a big curve not far from the Wycliff exit when I see a car spin out of control, jump up onto the median and slam against the guardrail. Their car is facing the wrong way now, but I can't tell if anybody's hurt and they hit pretty hard, so I pull my car over to the far right side of the expressway. I park about thirty feet in front of a '61 Chevy Impala. The man who owns this Impala is now darting across the freeway to render aid. I, too, want to render aid in a heroic manner. I walk between his car and mine as I try to spot an open space in the traffic; that's when I see a very large black woman in a very large blue and white '56 Buick go into a spin around that same curve. It happens fast and I freeze as I watch her big car spin once, twice, halfway around one more time and she's sliding sideways right toward the back end of the man's Chevy. Clearly, she's out of control and not likely to gain it within the next few seconds. She's going to hit the Chevy, and I mean, she's going to wham it, and hard!

That's when I realize, *What am I doing standing between his car and mine? Chances are, I'm about to be the crunchy-on-the-outside-juicy-in-the-middle part of this slam-sandwich.* I quickly take action without making a conscious choice to do so. I run backwards between my Toyota and the Chevy, screaming and pointing. The guardrail is to my left. As put my hand on it and vault over, I hear the crashing sound of car against car and then I fall head over heels. Almost I get my footing, but fall again and practically skid straight down on my elbows, chest and chin, then I rollandrollandrollandroll androllandrollandrollandrollandrollandrollandrollandrollandrollandroll androllandrollandrollandrollandrollandroll land roll. Clearly, I am out of control and not likely to gain it within the next few seconds. I rolland rollandrollandroll some more. *I'm going to die and end up in a ditch,* I think. Then I get to think about it again. *This is taking a really long time,* I notice as I rollandrollandroll the last few yards. *This isn't exactly how I saw being dead in a ditch* I whine in my head.

When I finally *whump!* against the curb at the bottom of this very tall steep hill with my arm splayed out onto the service road below the freeway, I have only enough wits about me to be grateful for having been stopped by the curb and that no vehicle was close enough to snap my arm in two. Then, as my wits stop rolling and settle down, I'm also extremely grateful I hadn't been on a bridge when I jumped because I never looked; I just put my hand on the rail and went over.

It takes a few seconds to gather myself and check for blood and broken bones. When I don't see anything worse than a few scratches, I begin the long, slow hike back up this steep son-of-a-bitch of a hill. Over my panting and grumbling, I can hear that a crowd has gathered up on top. Police are there, I can hear 'em talking on their radios. They've probably set out flares and the traffic must be slowed to a crawl. I see whirling lights and hear a police radio announce the ambulance is pulling away from the middle of Stemmons Freeway, but there's no siren sound so maybe the people in the first car weren't hurt. As for me, I continue to claw and scramble up the embankment, grabbing at weeds and tufts of dried grass until I can see some more.

Ooh, boy, what a mess. The lady's '56 blue and white Buick looks permanently imbedded sideways into the trunk of the man's '61 Impala. The woman who was driving the Buick does not appear injured. She's shaken - and shaking - but not hurt. The owner of the Chevy is quietly trying to explain to a police officer what happened He's pointing and making elaborate whirling motions with his hands and arms. The cop keeps shaking his head and rubbing on his neck like he's having a really hard time believing any of this.

"Are you sure that's what happened?" the policeman asks him again and again.

By this time I have scratched my way up to the guardrail; that's when I hear a woman's voice say, "So, then, whose little car is this?"

It's at this point I poke my head up like a prairie dog. I've got weeds in my hair and scrapes on my neck. I'm covered in dirt and there's a plastic wrapper of some sort stuck to my bloody elbow. I look spooky, I'm sure, and creepy, like someone-to-be-run-away-from.

"It's mine," I say, calmly, and crawl over the rail. The black woman screams and topples backwards into somebody's arms, but because this woman is so large, both she and the surprised man who catches her fall down. People rush toward them; other people rush toward me.

"Are you all right?" the police officer asks.

"Sure," I say, "of course. Why wouldn't I be?"

"Did you fall down this hill?" He points over his shoulder with his thumb toward the embankment.

"Jumped," I say. Somebody gasps.

The whole tone of the crowd changes as if I'm insane. They all stare at me. I stare back. "Look," I tell the cop, "It wasn't a suicide attempt. It was self-preservation. I thought I was going to get crushed between all these cars." I point to the Buick and the Chevy, which has been pushed to within eight inches of my bumper from the impact. I nod to the crowd like that settled the issue and sashay to my Toyota.

I fish my keys out of my jeans pocket, climb into my car, just as cool as I can be, start it up and motor on. I get past the traffic jam, level out on the freeway, and then the oddest thing happens. About three miles out, my legs begin shaking, a *bongbongbonging* kind of rhythm that I can't stop. They shake all the way to the lake; that's two whole hours worth of shaking. It's a shake I can't shake. I feel like a junkie - or how I think a junkie might feel when a junkie needs a fix.

I still have a bad case of the jitters when I arrive at our cabin. Everybody is glad to see me but due to my dirty condition they know something is up. At least, I think Mother and Daddy know, but I'm not sure and I can't stand the idea of upsetting them so I keep mum.

"What happened - you fall down? Get run over? Get drug by a horse?" Daddy asks me.

My mind takes off in a thousand different directions. Oh, how I want to tell the truth and burst into tears and have Mother hold me, but I just can't. We kids have an unspoken oath to never tell our folks we almost died. Almost dying is something I might tell them years from now, but not today. Today, I just make something up, something I know they'll go for and not question much. My legs start shaking again, though, so I walk around so they won't see. "Naw," I say, "I just got together with some friends this morning. We played a little touch football, that's all."

As I walk by Daddy grabs my elbow and examines it. "Shitfire," he says, "You just got the hell knocked out of you. You look like somebody needs to learn the rules of touch football. There's a reason it's called touch football, you know." He looks at the raw scrapes on my neck. "Well," he says, finally, "I hope your team won the game."

"Of course, Daddy," I nonchalantly tell him. "We always win. I played quarterback."

What I didn't say was, "I'm all right." Throughout our lives Mother told us that the words she hated hearing most were, "Mother, I'm all right." To her those words meant that something had just gone badly wrong; that one of us had just brushed up against the edge of death and was calling to report that we'd skirted past it once more. In the long run I don't know if the words, "Mother, I'm all right," were more comforting or as horrible for her as hearing, "Mrs. Seay, we need you to come downtown and identify your daughter's body."

Either way, our oath of silence was the offshoot of Mother's dread. To my knowledge, the only times any of us ever broke the code of silence was when it was absolutely necessary, and even then we tried to sugarcoat it as much as possible:

"Mother, I'm all right, but do you happen to know my blood type offhand?" or,

"Mother, I'm all right, but do you think the dentist's office is open on a Saturday night?" or,

"Mother, I'm all right, but remember the time you stitched up our baseball with embroidery thread; how'd you do it? ..."

Stuff like that. We all adored Mother. She worried enough. It was the least we could do.

"If A=success, then the formula is A=X+Y+Z,
where X is work, Y is play, and Z is keep your
mouth shut." - Albert Einstein

Chapter 17 – Good Luck / Bad Luck

"You just drive the car; I'll tell you where to turn!" I remember shouting that to my Mother one late afternoon in the spring when I was nine as we raced around in the station wagon. I was hanging my head out the window and the wind whipped at my hair. We were following a rainbow.

For an hour a rainstorm pelted Dallas but finally it cleared and now the sun was brilliant and golden, shimmering and liquid-looking, reflecting off the wet grass and trees like melted butter. Streaked across the sky in front of us was a rainbow of gargantuan size, bigger than any rainbow I'd ever seen. It was breathtaking and not very far it seemed to me - just right over there - beginning somewhere in the sky around God's sandals and ending, from my calculations, pretty close to the baseball diamonds at Kiest Park. That's where the pot of gold would be, I just knew it; and this time we would nail it, my mother and I, before anybody else had a chance at it. No family that I could think of needed a pot of gold more than we did.

When I was seven, I sprained my wrist falling off the back of Aunt Roxie's barn in Forestburg, Texas. It was not a very big barn - more like a manger, really - with room to store hay and oats, but tall enough to wham pretty hard if you fell off of it. I had climbed up on top to see if I could spot the end of the rainbow which seemed to have plopped itself down just beyond the rodeo pens. I was crying as Mother dragged me into the house to put ice on my arm - not because it hurt, which it did, but because she wouldn't let me dart across the highway and scramble through two barbed wire fences and a tangle of scrub oaks to check out the pot of gold.

Mother never popped my bubble about the pot of gold, though, something I've always been grateful for, and was a tremendously good sport about racing through the streets of Dallas, wasting gas, turning where I told her to, until the rainbow had disappeared along with the pot of gold. Even now when I see a rainbow, *what-if* still wafts across my brain like a favorite memory evoked by the scent of a certain rose.

For someone who came from a family so seemingly plagued by bad luck, I manage to stay surprisingly optimistic - most of the time. Maybe it's because I understand more about our energetic creation of good luck and bad luck now than I did before. Or, maybe I just finally understand the difference between luck and stupidity.

For example, when we were eight and nine, Dean looked down into a metal fence post and got stung right above his eye by a wasp. That was bad luck. When I did the exact same thing only seconds after he did and got stung in the eye, too, well, that was stupidity.

Or, when Mike climbed up on the neighbor's garage to retrieve a badminton birdie and slipped off and landed on the metal spikes of a cyclone fence, that was bad luck. When Pat chipped a tooth in a rock fight with a neighborhood bully, well, that was stupidity.

As young adults we still didn't grasp this bad luck/stupidity dichotomy and it almost got us killed. For example, when I stopped for some gas and a pee at a service station where a robbery was in progress, that was bad luck. When I grabbed the robber's gun and tried to wrench it from his grasp like I would have a cap pistol from my brothers, that was stupidity.

Or when Dean stopped on the freeway to help a trucker and wound up getting his legs crushed as a drunk driver plowed into the back of his car, that was bad luck. But when Dean got busted for selling marijuana, and, well, yes, that was stupidity.

Mother tried her best to downplay the whole selling-marijuana-thing. "There was only a tiny little bit," she claimed, "not even two ounces, not even a baggy-full, not even enough to get high on," as if she knew what two ounces of dope looked like, or what those two ounces would do to a person, or what it would sell for! *Yeah, right!* When Mother was in downplay mode I just rolled my eyes and thought, *And how many kilos have you hoisted in your lifetime, Mother?* It was, well, you know.

So I don't buy into the whole bad luck notion, if for no other reason than it bums me out. I don't want to dwell on bad luck when there's always the possibility of something better, something grand, the pot of gold at the end of the rainbow.

Hope springs eternal in the human breast, so I've heard, and I suppose my bosom is as good a place as any for hope to bounce around. It seems to do that a lot. It all started with my first box of Crackerjacks, truth be told, back when candy bars were a nickel and a box of Crackerjacks cost a dime. Mother, notorious for her ability to pinch a penny until it screamed and fainted, would sometimes relent and stop off for boxes of Crackerjacks on the way home if we'd behaved ourselves especially well in church that morning. Our payoff.

Even though I liked Crackerjacks, it wasn't the popcorn or the peanuts or the candy coating that made my heart flutter, oh no. It was the surprise inside, the hope - it was the possibility of what could be, the what-if that excited my heart. Just the chance of finding a terrific prize hidden somewhere in that avalanche of carbohydrates was almost more than I could bear. Oh, my head spun the first time I tore open the tiny envelope and revealed a cardboard game with indentations and almost microscopic B-B's to go in them. Never mind that the plastic bubble covering the whole thing burst almost immediately and the B-B's ricocheted all over the kitchen floor. Never mind that Mother seemed to find another one with her bare feet every two days for the next six months. I was hooked. I'd seen the prize and I'd touched the brass ring. If only for the moment, I'd lived in the possibility. In my chest I felt an exciting, wonderful, thrilling BOING. It felt like hope.

Mama Loyes won a plastic record player at my elementary school's spring carnival and my cousin Herbie won a car in a drawing once, but, beyond that, Lady Luck didn't lay a big smooch on my family. Maybe what Lady Luck usually laid on us was a down-home, back-behind-the-barn kind of smooch. Daddy felt lucky if the fish were biting and Mother felt lucky if the repairman could fix the washing machine - yet, again. She felt especially lucky if it didn't cost as much as she'd feared. And my whole family felt pretty lucky if the current Texas summer wasn't as hot as the last summer.

Nonetheless, like the annoyingly optimistic teaser stallion I saw at a horse breeding farm one time (who never actually got to 'do it' but was just there for the pre-game warm-up) there's something deep inside me that always thinks, *maybe today's the day*. Ahh, hope springs eternal and all. So, it should come as no big jolt that, yes, I am one of those suckers who enters contests, buys lottery tickets, reads her horoscope, and believes in fortune cookies.

At last count, I had six of those little fortune cookie strips in my jewelry case - more strips than jewels, actually. These are the really primo ones I've saved over the years to remind me that great wealth and staggering fame are just right around the corner. I believe that my fixation on rabbit's feet, four-leaf clovers and horseshoes could pay off any day now. And yet, gambling, as we normally think of it, holds no thrill for me. Poker seems rather dull and slot machines too impersonal. I've been to horseraces, but I don't care who wins. I cheer and squeal because the horses look so magnificent when they run. But I can't let a Wednesday or Saturday go by without plunking down my dollar for a lottery ticket.

When I was growing up in Texas there was no state lottery, the prospect was voted down every so often by people who thought lotteries were the devil's doin'. But when I fill out my lottery card each week, carefully choosing my lucky numbers, the tip of my tongue sticking out of the corner of my mouth, why, I don't feel sinful at all. I feel hopeful. And when I think of all the good I could do with a squillion or so extra dollars of disposable income, well, gosh, I feel absolutely righteous.

Louise, the lady at the grocery store who sells me my ticket each time, says, "So, whaddya think? This the one?"

I shut my eyes; lean my head back and hold the ticket to my heart. "Feels like it," I tell her. "You'll be the first to know, then dinner's on me." Our unspoken friendship is sealed with this pledge twice a week.

Of course, if I had a nickel for every magazine I've ordered out of fear that my sweepstakes entry would go into the wrong pile if I didn't order, well, I probably wouldn't need to win the lottery. As soon as they arrive, I plow into those big gold or white envelopes. I read and I hunt and I lick and I stick and I sign and I fold and I seal and I stamp, all the while wondering if mining for diamonds or drilling for oil in my back yard wouldn't be easier. It would certainly be quicker.

Heading out the door one day on my way to the bank, I spotted a man coming down the sidewalk just beyond the bushes. He was headed my way, striding forcefully like a man with a purpose. I swear, from a distance the guy looked so much like Ed McMahon it made my heart stop! *Oh, boy, this may be my best trip to the bank ever- what good luck!* That's what I thought. But when he kept walking and so did the little dog on the leash beside him, I realized it was just a gentleman who looked a lot like Ed out for a stroll. And when I stepped crooked on the edge of the walk as I continued to watch him, lost my footing, and tumbled into the junipers, well, that was either bad luck or just plain clumsiness. No pot of gold today, and not even the real rainbow, but, hey, there's always tomorrow! So, is it bad luck to believe in good luck? I say, "Never!"

I don't admit to planning my day around my horoscope, but if it's there is a horoscope available to be read, I almost always read it. And once I read the prediction I do try to fit the vague zodiac rhetoric into this specific niche that is my life. Usually, trying to unravel the advice is too much work and I give up. I'm looking for a horoscope that names names. If it doesn't have anything to do with revenge toward people I know are my sworn enemies, I forget the whole thing in less than ten minutes.

I suppose the day will come when my phone or doorbell will ring and I won't instantly think: *Ed McMahon!* or *prize patrol!* Maybe one day I can walk past one of those plastic eight-balls without asking a question and quickly turning it over to see my fate. But not yet. Because I still remember the prize, you see; and memories of that thrill keep bouncing around in my brain like B-B's across the kitchen floor. I've touched the brass ring, lived in the possibility, and I've never stopped thinking, *Maybe today's the day!* I've felt the BOING in my chest and then the flutter like a million butterflies are inside my heart. And you know what? It still feels like hope. Lucky me.

*"Family life is like a runny peach pie - not
perfect, but who's complaining?" - Robert Brault*

Chapter 18 – Food For Thought

A trip to the Farmer's Market is as good as a time machine
because, for me, memories are triggered by smell - usually food smells.
Today I stand across the stall of a farmer and accept the heavily
weighted paper sack. It makes crinkling noises as I unroll the top and
reach gingerly inside. Our eyes meet, the farmer and me, as I pull out a
perfect, homegrown tomato. The reddish-orange jacket looks about to
burst - a pinprick might send it flying around the market, sputtering like
the death knell of a birthday balloon. *How does God do this so perfectly
time after time?* I wonder, and rub the tomato's smooth, waxy skin
against my upper lip. Then I take a sniff. It's not the first time my nose
has taken me back to my childhood, back to Texas.

Although it seems to have sprung back to life in recent years,
when I was a kid, Mallard, Texas was practically an imaginary town.
Just memories and a cemetery at the end of a dirt road could prove it
had ever been there. My Aunt Vera and Uncle Charlie had a tiny farm
in Mallard where they grew a family and a garden and, finally, old
together through sixty-five years of marriage. I tasted my first
homegrown tomato there the summer before I turned ten.

It was a time in my young life when I had more energy than a
barrel of rodents on amphetamines, so spending part of my summer
vacation burning it off with various relatives who lived in the country
was a welcomed relief for both my parents and me. In 1959, I'd never
been any place cooler than ninety-eight degrees in the summertime.
Texas was a vacuous fireball, apparently having sold all of its air to
another state each July and August. You had to get up early to work in
the garden during a Texas summer or, as Aunt Vera said, "...you'd drop
dead in the corn before noon."

On this particular scorcher of a morning, Aunt Vera and I had been hoeing and pulling weeds. The garden seemed to expand another acre with each passing second. New weeds were sprouting in my footprints, chasing me down each row like heat-fueled vipers. *Life was over, I knew it.* Here I was, a nine-year-old girl on her way to meltdown. Soon they would find me, I was sure, only a blue t-shirt and red shorts floating in a puddle of melted child. I dropped my hoe and headed to the house for some water.

The well water Uncle Charlie had drawn earlier was still cool in the bucket and I was on my second cup when Aunt Vera banged into the kitchen in those low-top black Keds of hers and her big straw hat flopping up and down with each step. She carried a vanilla-colored bowl full of just-picked tomatoes that she placed on the table in front of me. With one quick swoop, she slid the saltshaker in my direction. Remembering my Mother's prediction of rattlesnake-sized parasites living in my intestines if I didn't properly wash my fruits and vegetables, I picked up the bowl of tomatoes and headed to the basin to rinse them. "No," Aunt Vera said, "these are better with a little of the earth left on." And she was right, of course. Great Aunts and Grandmothers almost always are.

There is a tree along the road somewhere between Forestburg and Mallard and each of the million times we drove past it, my grandmother would say, "Vera married Charlie in a wagon under that tree right there." I guess she really wanted me to remember it, and I guess I really didn't want to hurt her feelings by telling her I'd heard that story a million times already so I always acted surprised and impressed. "Really?" I'd say. "In a wagon!" And Mama Loyes would nod her head and point to that tree, secure in the knowledge she'd hammered home one more vital piece of family info - another link, some tidbit as crucial in the telling of family lore as a child's name or an anniversary date. And here I am, of course, telling the story one more time.

Aunt Vera and Uncle Charlie's wedding photo looked like a poster for missing children. The groom was nineteen (and looked about twelve) with a scrawny neck and a massive wad of wavy black hair that stuck out on the side of his head like some sort of Dairy Whip gone awry. His bride was fourteen (and looked about nine) with big brown eyes and a grim little mouth set firmly against any hardships yet to come, and there would be plenty. Three times they felt the piercing pain only a parent can know from losing a child. They lived through the Depression and then watched their only remaining son go off to war. Still, they never lost their thrill for life or for each other, and their farm was a sweet place because grandchildren and cousins and love filled it up from fence post to fence post.

As I age, it occurs to me more often that the most spectacular thing to remember about people is that there was nothing much spectacular about them at all. For it is in the act of remembering them, and the ways in which their simple goodness touched my life, that I honor them. And in honoring them, I bow to the privilege of carving my own initials in the trunk of our family tree.

Remembering is not a shameful thing, nor is it even always sad. I sniff the tomato once more and then hold it aloft, like a glass of champagne, for a toast. "Aunt Vera and Uncle Charlie," I say, "here's to you. Thanks for loving us all so much." And as the tomato's seeds squirt out onto my pants leg and the juice dribbles down my chin, I am thinking that we are all that is left - seeds and cousins bound together now only by genetics and memories, but all of us somehow better with a little of that Texas earth left on.

"I come from a family in which gravy is considered a beverage." - Erma Bombeck

Chapter 19 – Good Food / Bad Food

When my Aunt Edna passed away in 1999, our clan lost the last in a long line of what we called "the really good cooks". At her wake I explained to her granddaughters the reverence our family held for the women who cooked for us all our lives and who properly understood the importance of salt, pepper, sugar, butter and any other kind of grease in a southern diet. "Now, girls," I said in my best Texas accent (because they grew up in Virginia and they appreciate this) your grandmother was an extraordinary cook and the best pumpkin pie baker in the history of Texas. She knew how to make food melt in your mouth, no doubt about it. But your great grandmother, Mama Loyes, well now, she was the champ. She could make food melt in the air before it ever hit your mouth. Here's how Mama Loyes cooked: *Himmmmm...* she'd say to herself, *now, what holiday is coming up next? Oh! Thanksgiving! Gosh, it's already October. I'd better start the green beans.* Thanks to her, we only ingested vegetables the color of an army cot. They turned to mush on the short trip from the pan to the serving bowl.

Mother was a good cook, although not very creative, but only because we wouldn't allow it. We grabbed our throats and fell over sideways the night she put caraway seeds in the cole slaw and balked at anything we hadn't seen before at our table. She worried about our nutrition, however, which forced her to cook liver and onions once a month (which nobody liked) just out of guilt. I grew up in a lower-middle class neighborhood, so the comforting aroma of onions-frying-in-something in the evening was not uncommon. However, if the onion smell was overpowering, making our eyes tear up all the way out to the front yard where we were playing baseball, well, it made us suspicious. *This was clearly designed to disguise the liver, wasn't it? Was this a possible liver and onions night? Oh, God, please, No!* And we scrambled to see which of our friends would invite us over for dinner.

It was our Mother's concern over our nutrition that almost got me killed right in the middle of <u>The Ten Commandments</u> movie (which we saw every Good Friday at the Jefferson Drive-In for my entire childhood). Mother would not allow us to eat "that awful junk," as she called it, at the drive-in. She was sure it would kill us. So, we brought our own junk from home: King-Size Fritos, popcorn in a greasy grocery bag, and Kool-Aid in a thermos.

The twins and Peggy were asleep in the back of the station wagon and Dean was up at the playground right below the big screen - still a boy, but practicing to be a thug. I was bored with this movie since I already knew how it turned out; and, even if I didn't, it was clear Charlton and his gang was going to win. Again. *Ho-hum.* I had to keep quiet, though, because Mother stared at the screen practically bug-eyed as if she were witnessing a true miracle - and one she'd never seen before. Maybe she just had a crush on Chuck Heston; after all, she had raved about <u>Ben-Hur</u> for weeks.

Trying not to chomp too loud and wreck Mother's concentration, I managed to swallow a King Size Frito sideways, which slowly and agonizingly scraped its way down my throat, as if it had suddenly grown claws like a possum. It got stuck, going nowhere. And then it began to expand like an inflatable raft. I winced. I wheezed. I coughed, thinking maybe I could hold off trying to ask for help until Mr. Heston finished waving his arms at the water and booming "Let My People Gooooooooooo!!" in that God Almighty voice of his. *After all, I could hold my breath under water for long periods of time and this was almost like that - wasn't it?*

I briefly recalled, between bouts of gasping, Mother's pre-Heimlich maneuver once used to dislodge a plastic checker from my baby sister's tonsils: she had grabbed Peggy by the ankle, slung her up and popped her entire little body like a bullwhip. And I decided, *Now that I am ten, if Mother does that to me, it will surely break my neck.* I also thought, *If I mess up Mother's magical moment with Charlton*

Heston and the Ten Commandments over something as stupid as a Frito, she just might break my neck anyway. Clearly, I was in a bind.

I held off as long as I could. There was tremendous pressure behind my eyeballs. I tried to pant, but no air would come out. I hit myself squarely in the chest with my own fist, but nothing shook loose. *Here I* am, I thought, *only ten years old, not the first of my bunch about to die with grease and salt on her lips, but the first, I am certain, to do so at the drive-in movie.* Dying this disgracefully was not what I'd envisioned for myself. Finally, in desperation, just before my brain exploded, I leaned over on my side toward Mother, my eyes scrinched, my little hands clutching at my chest, my neck stretched out like a box turtle as I strained to give the Frito more room to get moving. Nothing was happening. "Moth-errrr," I croaked (Think: Wolfman Jack being strangled underwater and you can imagine how I sounded). "Shhhhh," she replied, waving her hand at me. Her eyes never left the screen.

"Moth-errrr," I croaked again, pointing to my throat. "Free-toe... stuck...hep...hep."

"Shhhh - what??" she said, finally noticing something was going badly wrong. I gotta say nobody could move faster than my mother when tragedy was about to strike. She grabbed me by the left arm and yanked it like a ripcord, pulling me forward. At the same time, her right hand whirled around and whammed me so hard between my shoulder blades that a glob of corn-mealy mush catapulted from my throat and arrived in a splat against the windshield only a nano-second before my nose splatted against it, too.

Mother handed me the thermos and two Kleenexes - one to wipe the windshield and one to wipe my nose. "Drink some Kool-Aid," she said, "the movie will be over soon." And she turned back toward the screen to continue her love affair with Charlton Heston.

If that seems a little too unsympathetic to anybody else, well, it doesn't to me. It was my Mom. With five children to worry about, she did what she had to do in each moment. If she spent a lot of time coddling us after each near-death experience, she'd never have had time for anything else. Besides that, she was a good cook (if you take away the liver and onion episodes) and that warranted lots of extra points. Much could be forgiven of the one who feed you. 'Good Cook' was a title of great esteem with us and our family was loaded with them.

Mama Loyes's sister, my Aunt Audie, was a no-nonsense gal and a great cook, but you had to be quick to enjoy it. There was no messing around, *nuh-uh*, not at Audie's house. While getting it set out on the dining room table, Audie would yell, "Okay, let's get it over with!" And we all had to sprint in there and eat as fast as we could and we had to keep eating or Audie would grab plates and head to the kitchen to wash up. It's as if there was a contest to see how fast the whole process could be done from the first scrape of the peeler across the skin of a russet potato to the last clinking sound of silverware dried and put away in that squeaky drawer. I halfway expected Audie to throw both hands in the air when she finished, like a calf roper in a rodeo, so determined was she to get it all done quickly before the buzzer went off. Maybe she thought that if her house-full of people had full bellies then it would force everyone to pipe down. We were a loud and rowdy bunch.

In the time of my childhood (the 1950's and '60's), if someone had pointed a finger at me and my relatives and yelled, "Dysfunctional family!" we wouldn't have known who they were talking about. Where I grew up, a dysfunctional family was one that couldn't tell a story or take a joke and we were a long way from that in all directions. We "functioned," we sure did, but the way in which we functioned would have supplied material for a couple of made-for-TV movies, a bunch of best sellers, and a Twelve-Step program just waiting to happen.

Although we had more than a few alcoholics in our clan, and seeing as how we were from the south in general and Texas in particular, we had more than a few good cooks in our clan just to balance things out. Good cooks and alcoholics, usually a two to one ratio, seem to go together in big families. I may be the only one in the history of man and womankind who's figured this out. Confrontation and interventions were rare back then, so the alcoholics stayed the same. The rest of us stayed quiet. And, for some of us, there is a high price to pay for the silence. That's where the good cooks come in.

Like I said, Mama Loyes was a champ in the kitchen and we all took great delight in devouring whatever she cooked. Knowing what I know now about nutrition, I'm surprised any of us lived past the age of twelve. She made the most heavenly cream gravy for her chicken-fried steak and what she called "independent" mashed potatoes - with enough lumps left in them that you had to admire their character.

She was a believer in fresh vegetables, even though they probably had about as much nutritional value as tire tread after she got through with them - cooking them her customary six hours and with a big chunk of salt pork thrown in for taste. This gene of hers, this pre-disposition for overcooking she passed along to my mother and they became the only two women I've known personally who could turn pork chops into leather-like pads of pork jerky. This was meat which had to be eaten with your fingers - at the risk of whiplash, I might add - simply because tearing at them with knives and forks was too risky for a table full of people. Somebody could lose an eye.

And what's for dessert? *Oh my heavens!* Dessert might be coconut pie so rich creamy it'd make your tongue jump up and slap your brains. Or Mama Loyes might serve egg custard all cool and slippery with fresh ground nutmeg on top. Her only "low-cal" dessert - called thus because it came with no icing - was a fresh apple cake loaded with chunks of apple and cinnamon and sugar. To make up for the fact that this cake arrived at the table naked, she served it warm with a slug of vanilla ice cream the size of a high-top sneaker smacked right on top. When she really wanted to pull out all the stops, though, my grandmother made her specialty, a three layer German chocolate cake, so rich you had to drink a giant glass of water along with it or run the risk of swooning into a diabetic coma.

I just wish we had used food differently. I wish it had been prepared as much to enjoy and nourish as it had been to stifle and soothe. In therapy some years ago, I traced back my serious bouts of depression and discovered a four-month pattern that had begun at about age eleven. This was right at the time my father's alcoholism started into full swing. To this day I remember the feel of Mama Loyes's stubby little bear's paw of a hand patting my back. "Aw," she'd say, "got the mullygrubs? Wh'ontcha let me fry you up a little piece of steak?" In order to make me feel "better", she could slap together a menu that was a cardiac surgeon's dream come true!

Nobody in my family had the vaguest idea how to talk about our feelings, but we all sure knew how to eat. So, whenever there was anger or upset or sadness - and there was plenty - what happened was we all got fed. And the bigger the upset, the bigger the meal, that seemed to be the rule. I realized, finally, how ingrained this pattern of stuffing down our feelings with food was the night after Mama Loyes died in 1984.

I sat in the rocking chair in the den at Mother's house. Only the two of us were there and we sat in silence, the sadness in the room as thick as Mama Loyes's tapioca pudding. Mother asked me, "Are you okay?" I said yes. There was an awkward pause and then she added, "Why don't you have a piece of chicken?"

Years of frustration exploded out of me, and I screamed at her. "Mother!" I yelled, "I don't need a piece of chicken - I need to be sad!" And then I felt awful. I looked at my mother, this woman who loved me so, who had just lost her mother who had loved her so. Lamplight reflected in the tears running down her cheeks. I walked over to the table where she sat, knelt down and put my arm around her. "I'm sorry, Mother," I said.

"I only wanted to help," she sobbed, sniffing. "I hate to see you so sad."

"I know," I replied. "Only this time a piece of chicken won't do the trick." And we held hands and cried, my mother and me, deep in the sadness, in the moment, in the lamplight, in the den.

I've spent years now unraveling my patterns around food. I wish I could say I've gotten it all handled, but that seems far from the truth. In fact, the lie has almost circled around on itself, bitten its own tail, and become the truth. I've forgiven the alcoholics, forgiven the good cooks; now I'm working on forgiving me, the hardest part of all. And I'm hoping my arteries will forgive and forget while we're at it. Because now I'm a grownup, mostly, and as I walk around with gravy stains on the bib of my life, I've learned to look at this trip through existence as lessons learned rather than pounds gained or lost. I've realized these lessons I'm here to learn are also designed to make me happy; to know and understand that care shows up in a thousand different ways. And I've realized now - after all these years - that what we were served way back then was so much more than what I thought it was. What the good cooks in my family dished up, in the purest, simplest way they knew, were great big batches of homemade love. And how could I not be happy about that?

*"I have a simple philosophy: fill what's empty;
empty what's full; scratch where it itches."*
- Alice Roosevelt Longworth

Chapter 20 – Thanks For The Memories *(Mama Loyes, Miss Inez, and the Whole Enchilada)*

Oak Cliff is a huge segment of my hometown, Dallas, Texas. It encompasses about a third of the city, making a horseshoe shape around the southern part of Dallas. Within the boundaries of this community there are really beautiful parts, really crummy parts, and okay parts. Over the years, many of those parts have exchanged places a time or two: neighborhoods have faltered, fallen into disrepair, and then, miraculously, been yanked back to life.

I grew up in an okay part. When I was in high school, though, many people from other parts of Dallas thought Oak Cliff was a neighborhood of knife and gun-wielding thugs on every street corner with shootouts each night. Perhaps they were partly right, but not on my street corner. Mother would have whacked them with a broom. My high school pals and I even began calling our neighborhood "Oak Cliff-Oh," because when people asked us where we lived in Dallas and we said, "Oak Cliff," they stared at us for just a moment, then quickly looked away. Then they said, very quietly, "Oh."

My part of Oak Cliff we called "Hungry Heights" but it was really the Westmoreland Heights area. Born in the post-World War II housing boom, Hungry Heights was one of the okay parts, I guess, a neighborhood of frame houses with asbestos shingles, swamp coolers, and always the smell of onions frying in something for dinner.

The neighborhood also had homemade ramps, hills, jumps, trees, bits and pieces of dangerous things, especially around our house. I was a very active, bruised-up, scraped up and scabbed over little kid. I took every double-dog dare my brothers tossed my way. Sometimes I made the jump, and sometimes I fell. I shucked my jeans back then and put on a dress only under a threat - and even then only at the very last minute to go to school or church, and once to the Ice Capades where I wore a Brillo-pad of a petticoat with jingle bells on it and a pinafore starched so stiff I had to bend it like a piece of cardboard to get in the Chevy. For me, getting all dressed up was a bigger pain than losing a dare; like being snagged in a trap of nylon netting and humiliation from which there was no escape. Except this one time.

My grandmother, Mama Loyes, made the date with me. "We'll go downtown to see a movie and out to dinner, just the two of us." *Wow.* Downtown Dallas in 1956 to a seven-year old girl was more than a big deal; it was much higher than the top drawer of anything I'd ever done in my young life, even if I did have to wear a dress. And, of course, I *did* have to wear one if I was to be in the company of Mama Loyes who never went downtown without a hat and gloves on and a half stick of Juicy Fruit gum in her purse.

In a misguided attempt at taming my curly wavy mess of hair, my mother forced me to spend the night-before-the-date tortured by Spoolies and bobbie pins. When the big day arrived, Mother unleashed my mop and it *sproinged* into a curly ball on top of my head. If the force of my hair had not been pulling my face up so tightly, it would have been easier to spot the shame I felt over walking around under such a hairdo.

Mother and I had already gone several rounds over my wretched petticoat and we were gearing up for another go 'round when she declared the argument to be over. "The petticoat will be worn," she ordered - and that was that! Mother did agree, though, to snip off the jingle bells since it was nowhere near Christmas and was, therefore, stupid-sounding. So, by the time we wedged me into the dress she'd starched and ironed as stiff as a road sign, we were both worn out and cranky, especially Mother. I was also transformed, however, from a fairly normal-looking seven year old into a child who suddenly looked startled and flash-frozen.

But, by God, I was clean. And dressed up. I just wasn't sure I'd ever be able to sit down. And the quarter Mother made me stick in my shoe for spending money caused me to limp.

"Don't go to the bathroom by yourself! Don't talk to strangers! Don't buy any candy that's not completely wrapped!" Mother yelled from the porch as Mama Loyes and I roared away from my house in her '53 Oldsmobile. Looking behind us, I could see Mother running out into the yard waving, so I waved back, even though I was really waving her back into the house to avoid risking any more embarrassment. *Gee whiz, it wasn't as if we were driving to Oklahoma or someplace where Yankees lived.*

"How long does a big movie last?" I asked Mama Loyes. I'd only been to see Flash Gordon serials at the Westmoreland Heights Theater and I'd been a few times to the Jefferson Drive-In where I usually fell asleep as soon as it got dark enough to show the movie.

"At least two hours," she said, "so be sure and go to the bathroom when we get there."

I wasn't worried about my bladder; I was worried about my butt. The prospect of sitting for two hours on a cactus bed made me feel faint. I devised another approach.

Slowly, slowly, with the fingers of my tiny right hand, I began picking away at the scab on my knee all the while nodding in agreement to Mama Loyes' yammering about the merits of good grooming. When the scab broke free and a trickle of blood began making its way down my shin, I set the trap by casually mentioning, "Oh this stupid petticoat scratched my scab loose."

Mama Loyes, ever practical and worried about her nylon seat covers, skidded the Olds to a stop and bounced the big car up on the curb as she leaned over and rummaged through the glove box for some Wet-Naps. "Take that thing off," she demanded - one hand in the glove box the other hand slammed the car into park and cut the engine - "and let's put the petticoat in the trunk."

And I am thinking *Yes! Hoo-rah-rah-yes! Jesus loves me!*

Mama Loyes continues, "And don't you dare tell your mother."

Was she kidding?

Now, the big date began in my eyes. No longer encumbered by thoughts of a scratchy demise, Mama Loyes and I motored downtown to the Palace Theater to see *Around The World In Eighty Days* or *Cinerama* or something more important than *Flash Gordon.* In truth, I remember almost nothing about the movie. No, what I remember most was the posh surroundings - crimson seats and gold swirled things on the walls, the soft, amber lighting - and the anticipation in the air, like something big was about to happen.

Well. Something big *did* happen. Miss Inez Teddlie, the very same Miss Inez who played at Burnett Field, was suddenly lifted up from the bowels of the Palace Theater on a platform and, outfitted in her beautiful long dress, she began to play the organ. The music boomed and wafted into the air. I was so thrilled, I thought I would pass out. Mama Loyes was sure I was about to throw up. This was the most awe inspiring thing I'd witnessed since my Aunt Roxie's neighbor, whom I'd helped care for after he was temporarily blinded in an unfortunate incident involving an outhouse and a black widow spider, could all of a sudden *see* again one day as I fed him Campbell's soup. Two miraculous happenings in one short little life - plus, I wasn't wearing that stupid petticoat either time. I was sure I must be the luckiest little girl in the world.

After the show and while I was still in a daze, Mama Loyes and I arrived at the El Chico restaurant in Oak Cliff on Davis Street. Our table was up the steps into the center of the main dining area, the circular room with the big chandelier glistening right above us. *My enchilada dinner is superb*, I thought so I told our waiter, "My compliments to the chef!" Our waiter, a tall, handsome man, bowed from the waist and then disappeared into the kitchen. "What service!" I gushed to Mama Loyes, turning back just in time to see the chef striding toward our table.

"Muchas gracias, senorita," he said, kissing my hand. Well, I blushed and grinned the goofy, snaggled-toothed smile of a seven-year old. What a time.

In my picture box, along with photos, letters and other treasures, I have a perfect, tiny sombrero. It is made of straw, coated in plastic, and on the brim is printed 'Cafe El Chico'. I have kept it now for almost a half century and I expect I'll keep it from here on out. It represents a memory I don't want to lose, so I keep it to remind me. And when I put the tiny sombrero on the tip of my little finger and spin it around, another miracle happens, one that I like so much. I see crimson seats and soft amber lights; I see Mama Loyes and Miss Inez; I smell popcorn and enchiladas and Juicy Fruit gum; I hear organ music so dramatic and righteous, that if I shut my eyes and hold the sombrero to my chest and I can feel the notes clinging to my heartstrings and the memories spinning themselves into gold.

Mama Loyes

"Money will buy you a fine dog, but only love will make him wag his tail." - Kinky Friedman

Chapter 21 – Holy Cow

The calf was dying, starving to death, so we stole her - that's all.

I don't know why the Mama cow stopped feeding her, and I don't know why the rancher didn't take care of her. All I know is that I couldn't have lived with myself if I'd done it differently, and I know now I wasn't supposed to. The options were limited to one. And I am grateful that despite hearing my mother's voice in my head - *For the love of God, Jody, you don't steal somebody else's livestock - that's cattle rustling - do you want to get shot?* -there was no question among the three of us, Rachel, Judy and me, as to what we would do.

We didn't consider ourselves Bad Guy cattle rustlers because we called the rancher and left a note left at the neighbor's. Then we lifted the calf's tiny, frail body over the fence, out of the pasture, and onto some straw in the back of the trailer. She was a life ebbing away, one that we could save, and so we did. We named the frail black calf Susie (after Susan Hayward in the movie, *I Want to Live)* before we'd made it back across the pass to Pagosa Springs.

After buying all the electrolyte solution we could find in town plus a few quarts of Gatorade, we squirted as much of it into Susie as she could hold - and then a little more than that. We kept feeding her until her eyes bugged and she let out a bawl. Not knowing what else to do, we placed her on some straw in the corral and waited for something to happen - a miracle, a thunderbolt, something - or even acceptance of the possibility of nothing at all.

It was the summer of 1984. Earlier that year, my mother had begun her downward spiral, flaming out from chronic emphysema and even though she'd rallied after one long hospital stay in the spring, we both knew on some deeper level that Death would be coming to call again soon. We'd only managed to slap his hands away from her door for bits of time. He would be back, oh yes, and I hated the thought. Watching this sick little calf grazing in the pastureland somewhere between Life and Death, I was reminded again of our duty to love without clinging and when it is time to let go, to do so with honor. And I thought of my Mom.

The sadness gripped my heart like a claw and I couldn't wrench free from it so I took off up the mountainside to find a place to pray. Buddy, the younger Border Collie, followed me. The strange part is that I didn't call him or coax him; didn't even invite him, really, and didn't notice he was there with me until I stopped and then he stopped, too, about twenty feet away. He glanced off down the canyon when I looked at him - he was practically whistling a tune - as if he'd been there all afternoon and I just happened to stroll past. *What does he want?* I thought. I turned away and began to climb again and Buddy followed from log to ledge to boulder. And he waited for me - patiently, belying his basic nature - each time I stopped to cry out my anguish into the canyon and to pray for help in healing the wound inside.

Then, without warning or preamble I understood. It came, as it so often does, like a whispering breeze or a reflection of light. Buddy the Border Collie *was* my help. He was my own furry little black and white acolyte, waiting twenty feet from each altar I chose, sent on this day to help me, obeying a voice deeper than the canyon, lighter than the mountain air. It was a voice my own sadness would not let me hear. Buddy was pulling angel duty and I understood. Peace settled like a butterfly in my heart. I looked at Buddy and he grinned his best goofy-dog grin, ears pinned back, and wagged his nub of a tail. Then we walked back down to the ranch like pals headed home from an afternoon hike.

In the corral where tiny Susie rested on some straw, Judy's horses were doing the oddest thing; and I have to say how odd this was because Judy's horses were basically snots. One had a penchant for stealing the others' babies away and the rest were biters or stompers and fundamentally ill tempered. It wasn't a fun group of horses if you want to know the truth, which is why what I saw made my jaw drop. They had gathered only a few feet away from this sick baby cow to make shade for her. As the sun moved, the horses moved, shoulder to shoulder and tight. It was a gigantic, equine sundial with each element doing its part, pulling angel duty for the afternoon. I heard a whisper in my head and again I knew *something special is happening in Pagosa Springs.*

Susie stood twice in the late afternoon and went down both times - hard. There toward dusk we thought she might die. We carried her to the barn and laid her on some straw and then we three found ourselves talking to this tiny calf about the courage and the space to live or to die. We massaged her and talked to her and loved her until long after dark, giving ourselves to the process of trying to save another of God's creatures who deserved a chance. Suddenly, Susie's tiny body jerked and shot something black and gooey out her backside and then, exhausted, she laid her head across Rachel's boot and slept. As we slipped away and back to the house we decided - and I don't know how the three of us came up with this - that if she lived through this night, she would make it. We had done our best. Something else we all knew, though, was that we had to be willing to let her go as much as we wanted her to stay. That's always part of the contract Life and Death bring to the bargaining table and no amount of wishing it to be different would make it so.

Daylight comes early in the Rockies and it did the next morning, sending golden streams of sunlight through the blinds, throwing halos and rainbows around the room as it reflected through a crystal hanging in the window. I scrambled from bed, pulled on clothes, settled for yesterday's underwear, and created a tornado of activity and anxiety like someone late for the bus.

Out on the deck the dogs were waiting for me, grinning their dog-grins with a secret hidden behind. "Come on, boys," I yelled and they knew exactly where I meant as they tore across the deck, around the corner, down the stairs and out to the barn, staying ten yards ahead of me the whole time.

Come-on,come-on,come-on,come-on, they said in their dog-voices as they raced and barked and yapped looking over their shoulders to make sure I was still there. They circled back rounding me up, making me hurry along. Border Collies doing their job.

In the dusty haze of the barn, sunlight shone on Susie's head, now held high and with clear eyes as she stood on wobbly legs. Before this day, I would never have imagined a calf to look determined, but this one did. Her black coat, so dull and dirty looking only yesterday, now glistened with life. I knelt in the straw and put my forehead against hers. "Oh," I whispered, "You are the most amazing little cow." And from somewhere on the softest side of my heart, from that place where all my important memories are held in velvet chambers, I knew I would never forget this time.

Rachel arrived with a goat's bottle and formula to feed the calf. Right behind her Judy arrived with steaming cups of coffee and chocolate chip cookies to feed us. We sat in the dirt and the straw and laughed at the silly dogs and the snotty horses. And we loved the calf and loved each other, and loved a life that could give us so perfect a moment - the chance to be cattle rustlers and pull angel duty all at once - and a memory that would never let go. And, oh, we were grateful.

After my mother died two years later, I finally started paying attention to my life. I noticed how much time I spend watching for perfect moments - the golden aura, the light in the eyes, the gentle touch of a baby's hand against my face. I noticed how, in my idealism, I so often expect those perfect moments to arrive amidst the fluttering of gossamer wings and ethereal-sounding music. Hasn't happened that way yet, even though I know I've been witness to many perfect moments over the years. But, just as I know angels surround us almost always and most of the time they look just like us, I also know that perfect moments seem to arrive in a most ordinary way. They can look like cowshit on my pants, smell like a barn on a crystalline Colorado morning, and feel, once again, as if the hand of God has brushed my cheek and startled me. I do not feel afraid, no. I feel lucky. And blessed. Holy Cow.

*"...man is the only kind of varmint that sets his
own trap, baits it, and then steps in it."*
- John Steinbeck, Sweet Thursday

Chapter 22 – House-Swarming

I like to consider myself a lover of all God's creatures, but I know in my heart this is a lie.

Swatter-armed, I am relentless in my pursuit of any fly stupid enough to venture into my airspace, particularly the cargo plane-sized black flies that breed in the Pacific Northwest.

Although I have no desire to kill them, mice and other rodents are no friends of mine and I will do my best to avoid them and shoo them away.

Snakes? *Nuhuh.* Don't even get me started on that notion.

And, even though it's been years since I've played softball and my arm's not what it once was, still, I feel certain that on a good day I could nail a roach with a sneaker at forty feet, no problem.

Now, I am not a slovenly person. Sure, I can make a mess and scatter stuff around with the best of them, but you won't find any dust or grime *under* the mess. And I don't like creatures that slither or scurry or scamper in my own personal arena. I am stingy about this, pretty much dug-in. Call me old-fashioned, but scampering, scuttling things can just go live outside, and I'll probably even feed them if they will.

This is not exactly how I grew up. We had critters of every sort living in our house at one time or another, in addition to the usual assortment of dogs, cats, rabbits and parakeets. My older brother Dean, at various times, kept a lizard and a snake in his room. "Just wait," I remember my mother yelling to Dean, "that thing's gonna wrap itself around your neck one night in your sleep, and in the morning you'll wake up dead."

My younger brothers kept a crawfish alive in a bucket of slimy, filthy water in their room for an entire school year - the thing lived on raw bacon tossed in there once a week, can you imagine? *Yech.* Even Mother, who'd wrestled with enough baby pee, poop and puke over the years to harden her to almost anything, was grossed out by the crawfish and its living arrangements. "Just wait," I remember her yelling to the twins, "you guys are gonna wake up with jungle rot some day." According to Mother, jungle rot, strangulation, and almost all other bad things happened after you fell asleep - no wonder it was always so hard for her to get us to even take a nap! But we never saw any jungle rot on the twins. (Actually, after a while, we never even saw the crawfish, but the bacon always disappeared pretty quickly, so our assumption was that it was eating.) The twins also had a white mouse for a time with which they terrorized Mother and our Aunt Edna.

The cute little *peep-peep-peeping* baby chick my sister got one Easter actually grew into a teenage chicken, sleeping in a box on top of the water heater at night; squawking and zooming through the house at low altitude during the day. It crashed into the bathroom wall one morning and drowned in the tub.

Me? Well, aside from the time my cousin Herbie's baby raccoon crapped in my armpit at the drive-in movie in Bowie, Texas, my personal experience with critters has been mostly dogs, cats, horses, and one very special calf. So, you can imagine my distress upon discovering that squirrels had moved into my attic. The darn things hop from the trees in the front yard, run along the wires to the house, peel back the screen to the outside vent, scramble inside to the attic and set up housekeeping - *boom* - instant condominium, just like that.

At first I spoke to them calmly, aimed a gentle voice at the ceiling, moved my arms in a placating manner, told them I knew they were just needing a place to get in out of the rain and that they'd be leaving soon. "Yes, indeedy, I just know it." I said encouragingly. Later on, I tried bargaining with them - okay, it was really a threat. "Move yourselves, your families and your friends out right now or I will chop down every tree in the yard and destroy your entire food supply for the rest of your short little lives."

It didn't work. And then it got cold and I thought, *heck, I wouldn't want to be up in a tree on a day like today, either,* and then as time went on, I just sort of got used to them, you know how you do. I started listening for their volleyball game to begin each morning at nine in the morning: *Poonk! scramble-scramble-scramble, BOINK, pause, poonk!* Every morning I heard squirrels working out. And whenever the game didn't start and the attic was quiet, I found myself worrying about them and wondering if they were sick.

On my tender days, I think of them as mine, or at least my neighbors, and it makes me smile to think we can co-exist so closely. On my tougher days, when I'm so sick of them I want to pelt the attic with moth balls or buckshot, I think of them laughing in that Simon-the-chipmunk way as they gnaw my electrical wires to shreds and braid them into a rug shaped like a walnut. And late at night now, when they scurry around, *thump-thump-thumping,* I imagine them in evening attire, drinking margaritas from long stemmed glasses, doing the Lambada until finally, all sweaty, they fall into each other's furry little arms to do the ultimate dance as old as life. Sick, isn't it? I know, I know; I really need to get a hobby.

All of this got me to thinking, though, about how often in my life various varmints have come along to share my space. Even though I've never felt close enough to have them snuggle in bed with me like I would my dog or cat, still, over time, I just sort of eased into it, got used to them, and even came to care for them in an odd kind of way - like my chiropractor's eighty-four year old Dad said about his own hemorrhoids, "I've had mine so long I've given 'em names."

I remember sharing a house with some friends in Denton, Texas a lifetime or two ago. The house was big and old; probably a beauty in its day, but by this time was in much need of repair and care. A lazy and argumentative Baptist church a block away owned the place.

Because the members of this church spent so much of their time feuding, finding a competent repairman among them was tough, almost impossible. I realized this the night it took four members of the congregation to retrieve the body of a rat who had "passed on" behind our heater in the downstairs bathroom.

As tenants, my housemates and I were rather sad the rat had died. During this bitterly cold winter in North Texas, we figured having rats in the attic was as close as we'd get to having insulation in the house. Problem was, we couldn't figure out how to get the rats to hold still long enough to do any good at warming the house and none of us was brave enough to venture into the attic with a big wheel of cheese. Actually, the rats seemed to provide a necessary part of the delicate "eco-balance" of this rambling, rickety old place; the weight of them probably kept the floors from buckling. It occurred to me one day, though, that if the termites ever took their teeth out of the wood in the house at the same time, I'd be standing in a pile of lumber and rubble with a big wad of rats on my head.

We had roaches, too, big honkers, but never in the places you'd expect, not hiding under the toaster or rendezvousing behind the coffee maker, not anywhere in the kitchen at all. No, our roaches chose to hang out in the linen closet downstairs, which soaked up a sizable leak from the upstairs shower (as much as our Baptists were fond of water and dunking people in it, they never managed to find the leak). In Texas, when a roach the size of your brother's foot shows up in your home, it is preferable to refer to it as a 'waterbug'; otherwise, the thought of it is just too appalling. For this reason, we preferred to call our roaches 'waterbugs'. Sometimes we called 'em 'Big Old Waterbugs' or even 'Big Old Nasty Bastard Waterbugs'. Near as I could tell, we only had three of these monster roaches - uh, waterbugs - and we named them, appropriately: Big Leonard, Big Bubba and Big Nicky. I wondered what they ate since we never saw them in the kitchen, but I had to assume their days were fun-filled and action-packed as they whooped it up in the bath salts and dusting powder. As long as they kept to themselves, I was willing to put up with them. (Truly, I'm willing to put up with just about anybody - even Communists, even fundamentalists - only if they agree to stay out of my way. I just really don't want 'em right in my face.)

We'd planned a party at the house for a Saturday night. It was the potential embarrassment of having uninvited Big Leonard, Big Bubba and Big Nicky attend the party that opened the door to the next life for our houseguests. I was up early that morning to go play golf. I did not expect my first practice swing of the day would be with a toilet brush to snuff the life out of the smallest of our three roaches. He had startled me. The terse note I left for my friends told the story:

HEY, EVERYBODY - I NAILED BIG NICKY WITH THE TOILET BRUSH IN THE HALL THIS MORNING. YOU MIGHT CHECK FOR BIG LEONARD AND BIG BUBBA BEFORE THE PARTY.

Maybe someone bopped them; perhaps the roaches could read, I don't know. They were certainly big enough for pre-school. At any rate, we never saw them again, nor any of their relatives, and we didn't miss them, either, I have to say.

Just as I know the squirrels in my attic will have to leave soon, maybe it was just time for the roaches to move on. I don't miss them now - don't get me wrong - but I do, just sometimes, miss the time when the place I called home had so much wrong with it that what kept it from falling apart was the joke all around it. I don't miss the feuding Baptists, either, who so much reminded me of the roaches in their ability to scatter at the first sign of trouble. But I do, just sometimes, miss my state of mind, an easier dimension then, which allowed me to laugh at the thought of gigantic, mutant roaches living in my linen closet and to listen late at night for the scurrying sounds of rats dancing in the attic during a cold, cold, *oh-so-cold* winter a lifetime or two ago in Texas.

*"Just drive down that road until you get blown
up." - Gen. George S. Patton*

Chapter 23 – Blooey!

If the TV Annie Oakley hadn't worn culottes, she would have
been my hero. I loved it that she could shoot a hole in a silver dollar
tossed high up in the air. I swooned when she hung from the saddle
horn at a full gallop blasting away at bottles balanced on a fence. It
thrilled me so to see her shoot over her shoulder - with a rifle or a
pistol; it didn't matter - at the bad guys chasing her as she raced away
on her sleek and handsome horse. But it was those culottes, *man - ugh!*
I didn't buy it. A real cowgirl would've had on pants; I knew it in my
heart. (I also had a problem with Dale Evans - that whole scene just
didn't ring true.) But, wow, did Annie Oakley ever know her way
around a six-shooter. That counted for something, which is why I
practiced my quick-draw maneuvers almost every day as a child. I
knew someday I could be as good as Annie Oakley; only I'd be a more
authentic version of her. I'd be in pants.

Playing cowboy was what my brothers and I did constantly
when we were little (except the time I did Jack LaLanne exercises with
Mother and was so sore I lost my "gallop" capabilities and couldn't ride
my stick horse for a week) Being cowboys was like a job for us. We
got up, ate breakfast, put on our cowboy clothes - jeans, boots, long-
sleeve shirts, blue jean jackets, gloves, neckerchiefs and cowboy hats.
Regardless of the weather, no matter how hot it was outside, even
thought the lava-like tar from the street glommed onto the toe of your
cowboy boot quickly and even though it was so hot you'd be stuck if
you and your stick horse loitered too long on the trail, we cowboyed-up
and dressed the part. To top off our outfits, we carefully strapped on
our six-guns, tilting the belt at just the right angle for the fastest draw
and tying the leather strap around our legs to hold it in place. Clearly,
having your gun flap around while you rode your stick horse was a
majorly bad faux pas, cowboywise. Everybody knew that.

For several hours, we loped around the neighborhood, winning cowboy fights with imaginary crooks or wounding our cache of stuffed animals before riding back into the house and handing those make-believe varmints over to Mother. She was the 'Sheriff' and she would thank us for our devotion to duty and then toss them under the dining table, which was, of course, the "jail." Then we'd gallop back outside to fight for law and order some more, or at least until lunchtime.

By the time I was eight, I had pestered my parents unmercifully for a B-B gun for almost a quarter of my life, but they never gave in, which was a truly wise and wonderful thing I realize in retrospect. Up at the ranch with a friend when I was ten years old and showing off I took a .22 pump rifle off the wall of the bunkhouse and lined the sight bead up with a spot just below the brim of my friend's cowboy hat. "Why, I could shoot you right between the eyes," I said, cocking the gun. Then for some miraculous reason, I turned and sat down on the edge of one of the beds resting the rifle across my knees. I absent-mindedly pulled the trigger and the gun went off - *boom!* - just like that. I shot a hole through the wall - was shocked, startled, couldn't catch my breath - I never expected it to be loaded, but kids never do. I shook for the rest of the afternoon

The closest our parents came to actually giving us a real weapon of any sort was the year Mother ordered air rifles out of a catalog for the four of us for Christmas. Peggy was just a baby, so she didn't get one. These guns looked like real army rifles and came with a tiny bag of corks, which we shot at each other and lost in about twenty minutes. No matter. The street beside our house was being re-paved and was a giant mud hole for months and months - blocked off, torn up, perfect for recreating World War II. We learned to jam the barrels of our rifles straight down at any moment and come up blasting compressed-air, jet-propelled mud balls at each other that hurt worse than a hornet's sting and left angry, pulsating red welts on us that lasted for hours.

Along with our rifles, Mother's trip to the Army-Navy store brought us helmets, Army packs, grenade belts, canteens and mess kits.

This was the motherlode of all Christmases for us, especially in terms of what we really wanted. Finally we had useful presents.

And it didn't end there. Mother kept a sock box on top of the dryer for all unmatched socks. There they waited, like fishermen's wives, for their mates to return. And the mates never did. Well, my mother shortened and re-stitched our grenade belts to fit us and then she took all of those forlorn, lonely little socks, rolled them into pairs, sewed a big loop of embroidery thread through the top of each and helped us hang our "grenades" onto our new belts. Was this a great idea, or what? *Lose your grenade? It doesn't matter! There are always plenty more where those came from!* Mother's ingenuity when it came to helping us create our own fun was really magical.

Of course, the question has arisen as to whether my mother's acquiescence in letting me dress how I wanted to (not always making me wear a dress) and play how I wanted (not making me play with sissy toys) contributed to my sexual orientation. I seriously doubt that one. When I was just a toddler, my grandmother became concerned that I never played with my few "girl toys.". They sat in a basket, mostly gathering dust, although some of them were adorned with bandages here and there to help them heal from the gunshot wounds I'd inflicted upon them. Cobwebs gathered around their arms and legs, dresses faded into some forgotten pastel hue, and there they sat, untouched by my sticky little hands. "Jo," Mama Loyes asked Mother, "don't you ever buy her any dolls?"

"I do," Mother replied, "but she throws them down and shoots them with her gun."

So, did my mother make me a lesbian? No. My mother made me happy. It was my genes that kept me most comfortable in my jeans.

My cousin Shirley, a girl to the max, was pleased to the point of a squealing euphoric fit the year she got a miniature grocery cart and dinky, fake boxes of Tide, Bisquik and such to push around in it. Heading out to play army with my new gear, U.S. Army canteen clanking against my hip, charcoal smeared across my face to complement my commando camouflage, all I could think was, *Boy, Shirley got gypped.* Good thing she didn't see it that way.

I liked going fast. Seeing how far I could go - at anything - and live through it, pushing myself to the point of exhaustion, broken bones and/or ripped cartilage was what I loved. So did all three of my brothers. Unlike them, though, blowing stuff up was never high on my list of things to do. Call me an old-fashioned girl. I tossed a firecracker once which blew off my cousin Herbie's hip pocket and singed his butt. That got me yanked sideways by my more-than-moderately-P.O.'ed-mother, then grounded for many days. Explosively speaking, that was plenty for me.

If ever asked in a survey: "What would you say is the major psychological difference between men and women?" I'd reply, "Boys like to blow stuff up." I don't know why this is true, and I worry that the entire gender has mutated badly because of this characteristic.

A cab driver in Tulsa who was also a Vietnam vet, once told me the Post Traumatic Stress Disorder from his Army days and a significant hearing loss hindered his ability to do much more in life than drive around. When he wasn't driving his cab, he mostly drank. Since he didn't want to be a drunk, he just drove his cab practically all the time. Cab drivers and people on airplanes seem to be willing to tell people almost anything. "What did you do in Vietnam?" I asked him - loudly. I should have known better than to start up a conversation with a shell-shocked, hearing-impaired man in a zooming cab with the windows down.

"Explosives," he yelled, "I blew shit up."

"Did you just love it?" I screeched at him from the back seat, even though I knew what his answer would be - all boys like to blow shit up.

"Yeah," he said, a big grin spreading like pulled taffy across his face. I could see him in the rear-view mirror. "I had to run a lot," he yelled; "I just ran from bridge to bridge, basically, with fifty pounds of explosives on my back. The load got lighter as I went along, of course, so it was to my advantage to use it all up." He glanced back at me but I could tell his mind was re-living the memories rather that driving a cab. "The weather was hot and humid," he hollered. "I remember that part. And the air was so thick and sticky I could hardly breathe. Gunpowder, dirt and vaporized blood - that's what I was inhaling all the time." He took a deep breath.

"My legs felt dense as tree trunks and I thought my lungs would give out. Running was hard, like trying to run through chest-deep-water. But every time I stopped, you know, I got to blow something up. *Sweet Jesus,* it was fun!" This must have been a terrifically swell memory for him because at this point he *whapped* the steering wheel with the heel of his hand so soundly it made the dashboard rattle and the horn honk. I gotta admit, his enthusiasm for explosions shook me up a bit. I began to consider bolting from the cab's back door the next time he slowed down and running away.

"It played hell with my hearing," he continued, shouting, "and I get weird during a bad thunderstorm but, yeah, I'd do it all over again."

See? I am not making this up. There's a little chink in the male DNA, something in the goofy twist of that silly old double helix that throws a cog in the whole works. I'm sure if you were to look at it through a powerful microscope on a rainy late afternoon when the clouds are the color of *gunpowder,* why, you'd clearly see it spells out the word, 'Blooey!' I think that's the problem.

All of the boys in my family fell victim to the Blooey*!* gene. Heading to the lake one Fourth of July, my three brothers and their friend, Charlie, had loaded the back of Daddy's pickup with enough fireworks to maximize our family's first-strike capabilities. Mike was driving; Dean, Pat and Charlie were in the back. They were zipping along the highway gearing up for their weekend rendezvous with fire and smoke and bombs bursting in air when one of them got the bright idea to shoot off a bottle rocket over the cab of the truck. (Did I mention that this is a really unattractive and not-so-smart male genetic mutation?) Mike never saw it because he was going sixty miles per hour. The rocket took off, went straight out and up into the air then screamed right back at them, landing in the middle of the truck bed and igniting the four hundred megatons of explosives surrounding them. *Boys, boys, boys...*

Dean was hanging off the back of the tailgate; Charlie dangled off the side of the truck as every type of exploding device imaginable caught fire, spewed sparks and flame before *ka-booming* and streaking up into the sky. Roiling black smoke billowed out the back and down the highway. Missiles of every description buzzed and streaked and hummed and sizzled and whined, racing past their heads.

Inside the cab, Mike, in his own little world, listening to skinny, depressed Jim Morrison and the Doors croon "...Riders on the storm..." was still driving full-tilt. He never bothered to check and see what that big booming noise was behind him (I can't say for certain, but this may have involved some use of that infamous 1970's medicinal herb, marijuana, although I'm not naming names, please understand, in case I am mistaken). He only slowed down when he saw hands slapping at the windshield from above. He thought that, perhaps, God had come for him. Come for him NOW - in a 1966 Chevy truck, on a two lane highway near Lake Texoma, Mike figured he was about to be snatched up, long hair and all, soon to be "...Knock, knock knockin' on Heaven's door..." Mike took his foot off the gas. But it was not God, it was only Pat, dodging sparks, flame and projectiles. He had managed to crawl up over the cab and was beating on the glass to get Mike to stop the truck. By the time they pulled off the highway, their arsenal had been reduced to a few loose firecrackers, a large amount of gunpowder residue, and a Chevy truck whose back end smoldered like a barbecue pit.

All Daddy ever said about it was, "Well, the boys got an early start on the Fourth of July." And this was kind enough and close enough to the truth to be the truth.

*"Political language is designed to make lies
sound truthful and murder respectable, and to
give an appearance of solidity to pure wind."*
- George Orwell

Chapter 24 – Germs / Rodents / Commies / Drugs

In my mind, the laboratories at the Center for Disease Control are tiny, the size of walk-in closets, only not as nice, not carpeted, and without as much storage. There are only three of them. Inside each of the teeny labs is one short, hunkered, balding little man with thick glasses and dandruff. His name is never Chuck or Biff or Bo. His name is Wendell or Maurice or Lawrence. (Lawrence still has a bowling shirt from his college days with "Larry" stitched above the pocket. He even drank a couple of beers during the tournament finals, but had to sleep in his car.)

Although these three men don't look it, they are killers. Their job all year, every year, is to kill as many mice and lab rats as they can with various strains of influenza virus. Mother, terrified of anything rodent-like, would have loved these guys. Beyond Mickey, I'm not too fond of mice myself. Actually, any critter for which the term "scurry" describes how they move just gives me the willies. For Wendell, Maurice and Lawrence, though, it's competition, you see; the one with the most dead rodents wins the prize, which is dinner at the local Mongolian Barbecue restaurant, *Genghis Unleashed!*

Dead vermin and dinner out notwithstanding, what this competition really does is identify which influenza virus is the most deadly. It is actually very important work. The top three most dangerous strains are then isolated and vaccine is produced (if nobody in the government - and you know who you are - drops the ball) to inoculate the citizens of the United States who choose to inoculate themselves. It's a simple system.

Usually, Wendell, Maurice and Lawrence are right on the money about the top three deadliest influenza strains; sometimes they are not. In my lifetime, I can remember four years in which they were not. In two of those years, with much urging and badgering on my part, my mother got a flu shot and came down with the flu. To her, it felt like a trap, something the Commies had thought up to take all of us Americans down and, just to break her heart, I, her oldest daughter, was in on the whole scam. *I should have known better than to let her read Time Magazine, The New Yorker, National Geographic!* That's what I'm sure Mother was thinking. *My daughter's a liberal, a Commie!*

Well, she was half right. I am a liberal, and I'm also a firm believer in flu shots. The value of these we have only begun learning in the past decade, really. Flu shots weren't around when I was a kid. You got the flu, sister, you just had to tough it out. Not being all that tough to start with, I decided not to get the flu, and so I didn't. I just stayed in constant motion. There wasn't a flu bug made that could hang onto me long enough to take root.

I'm slower now than I was as a kid, so I have to be more cautious. This is why, ignoring the notion (inherited from my right-wing Mama) that any attempts at public health care are all part of a Communist plot, I get a flu shot. *Yessir*, I plunk down my $25 bucks each year and get popped with vaccine at the drugstore by a woman who swears to me she is a Visiting Nurse. "Visiting from *where?*" I always ask, squinting through my left eye. Then I make her say the Pledge of Allegiance just to be sure. (I may be liberal, but I am my mother's daughter.)

It is not a bad feeling, having power over influenza - especially since the strains seem to keep getting scarier. Except for this latest one, the Avian Flu doesn't sound too bad. It sounds like an aristocratic boy-detective, don't you think? *Oh, Avian, I just knew you'd be the one to solve this crime!* Even the influenza names are getting worse: The "Reefer Madness" strain from Panama, the Beijing "Ooh Mao Mao" Strain, and (my favorite) the Texas "Honky-Tonk Bar Fight Strain". What with Texas being my home state and all, it got me to thinking about the year Denton County almost collapsed on itself from the weight of Vicks Vap-O-Rub alone. Even now, I experience déjà vu at the mere whiff of Robitussen as I recall the winter of '84 when everyone I knew and everyone I didn't know in Denton, Texas had the flu. It was vicious. Kleenex was everywhere - a snowy blur of white, blue and pink tissues all over the place, all the time. Phlegm flew at random. Random ducked, I hope. It was awful.

Cinch up your bathrobe, slide into your slippers and pad with me now down the tissue-strewn Memory Lane. Wash your hands and then try not to touch anything. It is the winter of '84. As I said, everybody in Denton, Texas is sick with the flu. Except me. I am remarkably, luckily, disease-free, a quirk of fate I attribute to clean living and a fondness for onions. Okay, maybe it was just the onions. (When asked how to make a chocolate pie, I always say, "Well, first you take a big, ol' onion...") And, since I am in good health and a good friend, I feel it my duty to care for everyone. I starch a white napkin and pin it to my head. I am Florence Nightingale in Levi's; Gunga Din in a Mazda.

Unencumbered by sodden handkerchiefs or extra phlegm of my own, I race around town delivering medicine, soup, and messages of hope. Zoooooom! Over to Mark's to whap on his back ... Zoooooom! Over to Donna Ruth's to drop off her prescription... Zoooooom! Back home to whip up another batch of soup when the phone rings. It is my friend Diane, an I.C.U. nurse. She can barely speak. "Get me to a hospital," she whispers.

"Yours?" I ask.

"Oh, God, no," she replies, "Those idiots would kill me."

By the time I arrive with soup and medicine, Diane has changed her mind and her pajamas and will tough it out, she says. She's a true Texan. I grab a beer from the fridge and crack it open for her since she has no strength and cannot make anything resembling a fist. A pull-tab is out of the question. She leans back on the couch to wheeze, sip a beer, and watch *Hawaii Five-0* re-runs. "Book 'em, Dan-O," I say to her on my way out the door. Diane waves good-bye without looking back. I drive off with tears in my eyes, overcome with her courage.

I zip over to my friend Sheryl's house, find her spare key and let myself in. The gas stove in her living room is cranked up to the place on the dial that reads, 'Dante's Inferno'. It is nursing home hot in there. I bang one of the dining room windows open a bit just to let in some fresh air and head for the kitchen.

I am dropping globs of Vick's into a pot of boiling water when Sheryl emerges from her bedroom. *Oooh, man. This is rugged.* I try to smile at her and appear cheerful, but this is the worst I've ever seen anybody look who is still mostly upright. She looks crimped, pinched in the middle, possibly stabbed with something. Her hair appears to have been whipped in the Cuisinart and her eyes have begun to liquefy. She can't focus and weaves around the kitchen banging into cabinets. A used Kleenex clings to the one sock she is wearing. "Call my doctor," she croaks, flinging a scrap of paper my way, "I need to see him today." She shuffles and limps back to bed, groaning. I consider buying a gun to shoot her and end this misery. *Her family would understand,* I think. *Her Dad's a rancher and her brother's a Veterinarian. But there is no time to go gun-shopping now; I have lives to save!*

I call Sheryl's doctor's office, only to find out he is also her gynecologist. *Uh-oh, wrong end.* "Sorry," the nurse chirps, "but the doctor is only doing Pap smears today. Maybe she can come in next week."

"But you don't understand," I say, "I've got to get my friend in to see the doctor today," I say, "She's really sick with the flu."

"Nope," she cuts me off. "Won't happen today. Only Pap smears today."

"Listen," I hiss at her, "Sheryl's Pap is not the problem - it's her lungs. She is really sick, she can't breathe and I'm afraid she's going to die in the next twenty minutes if we don't do something. And if she *does* die in the next twenty minutes, I'm going to load her body in the car, drive to your office, and dump her in your waiting room. That ought to clear out the doctor's schedule, don't you think?" The nurse gasps. "Look," I continue, "just tell your boss that Sheryl will lie on the exam table upside down, fling her arms up through the stirrups and say, `Aaaaaaaah'. He won't even have to use a speculum." The nurse is not amused, but we get Sheryl in to see the doctor at three p.m.

The capper to the whole week, though, and my revelation, comes that evening as I lug my friend, Barbara Jean, up to the drugstore for some cough medicine. The place is packed with a mucous-producing crowd of sick people: housewives, cowboys, jocks, hippies, and everyone in between. All of them stagger around looking for that perfect cough-stopping, headache-ridding, fever-reducing elixir that will get them well or make them go unconscious until this is all over.

I read the ingredients on each bottle loudly to Barb, whose ears have been plugged since Tuesday. Her knees have buckled and I am holding her up. She is leaning on my shoulder, whimpering, breathing flu germs down my shirt collar. *Yech.*

"Awww,geeez," she whines in that flat, nasal, Minnesota voice of hers, "all of these bottles say 'Non-Narcotic'. Don't they have anything narcotic?"

The hippies yell, "Right-On! Narcotics!"

The cowboy looks up from the coughing fit he's having into his bandanna to shake his head yes. He is really struggling, trying to talk. It's not working "NARCOT...coughcoughcough ...NARCOT...coughcoughcough...NARCOT..."

"NARCOTICS?" I ask him, finally, and the cowboy gives me the thumbs up. *It could've been worse,* I think. *He could have used a different digit.*

The housewife, a tiny woman in a parka who looks like she's been hanging on a nail in the garage all week speaks up, but her voice sounds scraped, like something big and mean and is holding a grudge has her by the throat. "Narcotics would be good," she says. "Maybe if I'm lucky, I'll O.D."

All at once, I understand that my mother was wrong. *Flu shots have never been part of a Communist plot. Influenza is the Communist plot - the Russians want us all to be drug addicts! Eureka!* I slap both hands up against my cheeks, letting go of Barb who begins sliding to the floor. I grab her and yank her back up to my shoulder.

"Wha' happened?" she mumbles. "Did I pass out?"

"We have to leave," I tell her. "You don't want to be a Communist, do you?"

"Not today, I guess," Barb says. Then she brightens. "Unless being a Communist will get me some narcotic cough medicine..." I drag her out of the store.

Well, that was over two decades ago and a lot has happened. My mother died, then Russia sort of fell over on its side. I got the flu a whole bunch after that regardless of how many onions I ate. And so finally, drawing on a pool of good sense not often associated with my family, I began getting a flu shot each year. I think I am a better person for it, smarter, and with a better smile. I feel confident, unafraid of small-talk at parties, even powerful.

Powerful is a cool feeling. Last week a woman staggered into my office snorting and coughing. Rain dripped off the wide brim of her hat. She looked like hell, really whammed, like somebody had bonked her on the head with a board. Her voice sounded like E.T.'s. "Don't get too close," she croaked. "I might have the flu."

I stepped boldly forward chuckling to myself and felt the big "S" start to form on my chest - or maybe my bra. I got right in her face, daring fate. I could hear the Texas influenza bug trying to carve another notch in its gunbelt, but it wouldn't nail me, nosirreebob. Not this time. "Listen," I said to her, "I got a flu shot. So, unless you've got kryptonite in your pocket, sister, you...can't...hurt...me!"

She seemed vaguely disappointed, really, but I think that's because misery loves company. It's no fun feeling crummy unless you know you have the potential to make others feel as lousy as you do.

I'm not playing that game, though. I'll just keep getting my flu shots each year, if not to hold the Communists at bay, well, then, just to keep Wendell, Maurice and Lawrence busy. I like to look at it two ways. I'm their job security gal. And they are my rodent control men.

*"Courage is being scared to death and saddling
up anyway." - John Wayne*

Chapter 25 – Looking for Moose *(In All the Wrong Places)*

"It is not about being sick! It's about being terrrrifiiiiiied!" I
finally shout to my friend Elleen over the din of the floatplane's Cessna
engine as we soar up and up into the sparkling Alaska sky toward Mt.
McKinley.

Elleen has just noticed that my face has turned the same icky
color of white (ecru, actually) as my knuckles. "Jody, is something
wrong?" she asks, probably concerned I am only moments away from
heaving into her backpack.

Heaving is not the problem, of course, for I would quickly own
up to being sick. But admitting to all-encompassing, gut-wrenching,
anal-tightening fear? Well, that's a whole `nother kind of dog. At this
moment I cannot recall how I got myself into this mess - most likely
the very same thought Will Rogers had just before he and Wiley Post
fatally *splooshed* their floatplane into one of Alaska's lakes back in
1935. After all, when Elleen said, "Wanna go to Alaska?" and I replied,
"Sure," all I really wanted to do was see a moose. I didn't know it
would involve risking my life.

People with no fear of heights don't understand my terror. They
peer over the sides of really tall things, shouting, "Cool!" and "Far out!"
and (worse) "Hey, Jody, come take a look at this!" And when I
mention, again, my fear of heights and flying and such, they swat my
arm and say, "Why that's silly! There's nothing to be afraid of..." Or
they get a puzzled look, like a puppy, cocking their heads as they ask
me, most sincerely, "But how can you be afraid to fly? Don't you spend
a lot of time on airplanes?" Well, yes. I do. My work takes me to Dallas
and to Tulsa every few weeks. On these trips, though, I fly on great big

jets with cushioned seats which double as flotation devices. The pilots all have manly, sturdy-sounding names like Chuck, Jim and Bo. Even women commercial airline pilots have calming names - Elizabeth, Deborah, or Margaret or Jan - names that sound like the name's owner has some brains and grit and could figure out how to get us out of a tight spot; these are strong woman who are not afraid to slam a terrorist into a bulkhead and land a jet on the freeway. See what I mean? I think a woman pilot named Kiki or Brittany would make me nervous, that's all. Call me crazy, okay? Also, on my trips I am fawned over by swell flight attendants who give me snacks, decks of cards, and a pillow for my head. Sudden loss in cabin pressure? Hey, I want folks around me who would know what to do.

Not only that, never once on any of my trips have I ever even glimpsed an altimeter dial, at which I am now staring with such intensity that my eyes have begun to bug out and whirl around in opposite directions. *Ohmygod, I have suddenly become Marty Feldman.* Up and up and up we go, heading toward infinity, determined to carve our initials in the side of North America's tallest peak - or - leave skid marks across God's beard, whichever comes first. The *ba-BOOMing* sound my heart is making against my chest wall is muffled by the rattle of the plane's metal siding and I hear my Daddy's voice in my head: *"Know what I always think every time I fly? I always think,' The lowest bidder built this sonofabitch.'"* (More comforting, fatherly words of wisdom from the mouth of Texas Instruments' Methods & Tooling Engineer, Warren Seay, who flew exactly twice in the thirty-two years I knew him.)

Don't think I don't hear Mother's voice, as well. In 1985 I flew to London for a week even though I was terrified of flying that far over water. To prepare, I got myself hypnotized. Well the *booga-booga* factor wore off over the North Atlantic so I just got drunk. I was still terrified, sure, but I was really funny about it - at least, that is my hope. Anyway, while I was away, the engine on a Southwest Airlines jet fell off (they circled back, made an emergency landing at Love Field and everything was fine). A couple of days later, a small plane crashed up by Lake Texoma. As soon as my big jet landed back on Texas soil, I called Mother. "Oh, thank God," she said, "they've been dropping out of the sky like rocks."

Now, rattling around in this dinky Cessna up in the Alaskan sky, I don't want to cave in to my terror but it's hard to shake Daddy's voice and Mother's fear from my head. Instead of heavy metal and rivets, I feel like I'm surrounded by cookie sheets and a lawn mower, held up in the sky by tiny screws, duct tape, and some lucky form of Karma (certainly not mine). It's probably David's karma, our sweet, Shiny-Karma-looking-middle-school-aged-boy-pilot, who is busy spouting statistics and vectoring and such. Or maybe it's Elleen's karma. She's busy yelling, "Whee!" and "Hoo-boy!" and slapping my shoulder in a comradely fashion each time we lurch up another thousand feet and the wind bucks us around. I am straining to be nice to her, but it is more than difficult. I may have to shove her out of the plane.

This experience harkens my shrinking, quaking little memory back to 1988 when my pals and I jumped on the ski lift up at Mt. Hood in the summertime just to take in the view from the top. I've been up on ski lifts before without too much angst, but as I glance around, with the twenty or so extra feet of snow now melted, well, the ski lift is much higher off the ground than I've ever been without being surrounded by American Airlines. Riding along with my friend, Judy Weiland, I suddenly start to sweat and panic. *We are really very high up off the ground. Shit. Shitshitshitshitshit.*

Poor Judy - my hero - she senses my fear and not knowing what else to do, Judy begins chattering away like a magpie about work, relationships, sex, movies, about how she never really thought she looked good in brown until she started driving for U.P.S., about the approximate number of packages her truck can hold three days before Christmas and how excited people are when they receive a parcel. My hero jabbers about anything she can think of to distract me and keep me from jumping and just ending this torture.

I try to listen, honestly, I do, but my brain has suddenly become a food processor with somebody punching the 'pulse' button over and over. I can't unscramble what Judy is saying to me as the words whirl 'round and 'round in my head. On my face is that same stricken, anxious look I am certain I have whenever I am double-parked. *We are screwed, I know it.* Grasping the skinny metal bar holding us into the seat, I realize my hand is so sweaty that I have no grip of any consequence, certainly nothing sturdy enough to keep me from slipping right out of this thing and crashing down the side of Mt. Hood. *It is a girl's grip. Shit. I hate this.* Nonetheless, I squeeze the bar so tightly I create a bulging knot in my right bicep and I have the strongest urge to let my tongue flop out of my mouth and just hang there while I pant like a big St. Bernard; I don't know why.

As we pass one of the workers halfway up the mountain, Judy shouts out that we need to disembark and that we must do so quickly. The woman radios another worker further up. By the time we swoop in toward the hut, the young woman is out on the deck, trying to yell in a calm voice (as if that is humanly possible). "Can you swing the bar away from you? Can you just step out?" she shouts. Of course, I can do none of these things. I am frozen in place and not breathing, almost catatonic. We are about to miss our chance to escape, but there is nothing I can do except swallow and prepare to die. At the last instant, though, Judy sees that the saving of us is not up to *us;* it's up to *her.* *Thank God.* Judy flings the bar away from us, grabs my t-shirt and yanks me out with her as she jumps. We fall out sideways, about an eight-foot drop, but both manage to land on our feet. Oddly, somehow, I feel triumphant - don't ask me why. Judy and I stand there looking like characters in a made-for-TV movie as the skimpy little ski lift seat swings and squeaks, *backandforth-backandforth-backandforth,* in the wind as it heads up toward the top of the mountain.

Well. That was then. But now, here we are in Alaska so I push the memory of my ski lift experience to the back of my brain. It's crowded back there in the scared part of my brain, I know. We fly on. We look out the windows. I try to ignore the wreckage of a little red airplane lying way, way down there on the canyon floor. *Why, oh, why do I do things like this to my scared little self?*

After a couple of swoops around the south face of Mt. McKinley, we head down through the glacial gorge. Pretty spectacular, I must say, but no moose here. Moose up this high would have nosebleeds. Further down, we spy a goat on a cliff, clearly a loner, probably not very popular - a bad dancer, maybe, self-conscious and unsure of himself. He appears to be wearing earmuffs and has a grim expression on his face. (Never having actually *seen* a mountain goat in my life, I don't exactly know how their faces *should* look. All I know is that this one looks grim, okay? Not pensive; not angry; just grim.) I wonder to myself if he is also afraid of heights and if he would be interested in joining the support group I plan to start.

And then while heading back, we spot one - a girl moose sunbathing by a pond. She is alone - a spinster, perhaps, or just an independent gal who prefers her own company. Could be she's been heart broken one too many times. It is hard to say. Through binoculars, I notice her discreetly placed tattoo that reads, "Born To Chew Cud". Her swimsuit label sports the words, 'White Stag'. She is not very pretty, looks more like Joe Camel than is helpful, although I am willing to concede that she probably is attractive in a moosely kind of way. Maybe she and the goat will become friends, crossing all sorts of stereotypical boundaries high above the timberline - who would know?

"Wow, we found you a moose," Elleen exclaims and I nod. "Wasn't this worth it?" And I force myself to nod again. "Hasn't it been a blast? I'm sorry it's over."

Over? My stomach clenches. *That means we are about to try to land.* As if on cue, the plane lurches to the side and bolts back upright, but it's only sweet-little-David tipping our wings to majestic Mt. McKinley before he flutters on down to the little lake in Talkeetna to land. Every part of me is either crossed or tightened into a knot. I am grinning in a forced, idiotic-looking smile, pretending this is fun. I suspect my molars will shatter soon. Finally, we zoom in for a landing, the water rushing up towards us like it has a life of its own, like the waves are reaching up to grab us. Then the *whooshing* of the pontoons on the water coordinates perfectly with the sputtering sounds my anal sphincter muscle makes as it unties itself (luckily nobody else is aware of this). *Phew.* I can only stand so much humiliation before I feel it my duty to somehow end it all.

Back home in Oregon, I know my trip to Alaska has changed me. In addition to sporting a white eye patch like Wiley and spinning yarns like Will, my personal challenge is to see how many times I can use the word "vector" in conversation, especially at parties. The most significant outcome of my trip, however, is that I've written a book about the experience called <u>Fear: A How-To Manual - Scaring the Bejabbers Out of the Inner Child Who Needs to Grow Up Anyway</u>. Proceeds from the sale of my book will go toward financing my new business, Fraidy-Cat Adventures. No Burly-Girl stuff here, no way. At Fraidy-Cat Adventures, all participants will meet at my house for an entire year. We will kick back in big, cushy Barca-Loungers and munch our way through huge bags of potato chips while sharing with the group all of the terrifying things we almost did.

"So tell us now, Jerome, just how did you handle it when all those jerks in the pool were yelling, 'Chicken On The High Board!' Did you succumb to their taunts? Or did you wise up?"

We will punch each other's arms in a congratulatory manner and yammer on about how smart we were to have used our common sense and said, "No! Are you nuts? A person could get hurt doing that!" before we did something really dumb.

Then, after our meeting, we will all sit around feeling smart and brave as we channel surf with the remote until we find an old episode of <u>Northern Exposure</u> or even <u>Wild Kingdom</u> episodes on TV *(oh, to see Marlin Perkins wrestle that anaconda again - yeah, buddy!)* Of course, I realize all of these shows will be reruns and some members of the group may have already seen them years ago but, hey, I'm a livin'-on-the-edge kind of gal, and that's just another big old fat risk I'm willing to take.

*"There is no need for temples, no need for
complicated philosophies. My brain and my
heart are my temples; my philosophy is
kindness." - Dalai Lama*

Chapter 26 – Heathenism

"Mother's religion," as we came to call it, crashed and swirled itself into our lives on the night of a tornado warning and played havoc with all of us from then on. From that moment forward, we could not have been in a worse mess if the roof had blown off our house and cartwheeled down the street. And nobody will ever change my mind about that.

That raging, stormy night is still vivid in my memory. I can recall the downy feel of flannel pajamas - my own and my brothers' - as we entwined like a basket of cats trying to sleep on pallets of quilts Mother had fixed for us under some contortion she'd made of the twins' bunk beds. Like petals on a daisy, our legs fanned out, all of us forming a protective circle with our arms around Peggy who was just a few months old. Daddy was working nights at Texas Instruments so it was Mother's job alone to figure out how to keep us safe.

This was not easy. Violent bursts of wind lashed at the chinaberry trees in the back yard, bending them like soda straws. Goblet-sized raindrops *shplacked!* against the bedroom windows sounding like grasshoppers hitting against a windshield. From somewhere in the distance, Civil Defense sirens wailed, warning all of us in Dallas and Tarrant Counties to get down, get under something, get to a storm cellar, try and get safe!

For us, try-and-get-safe was under the bunk beds. For Mother, it was hunkered over the small round oak table in the den, squiggling the big black dial with gold numbers back and forth on our titty-pink AM radio. Despite the static and the occasional blast of mariachi music coming from one of the border stations, she kept at it, wiggling the dial like a safecracker.

Occasionally, forgetting the looming possibility of her family's demise, Mother would pause on some sports station out of Chicago to hear the baseball scores, astonished that the signal could make it all the way to Texas. "Gosh," I heard her say, "All the way from Chicago, Illinois." Mother had been a Dodgers fan as long as they were in Brooklyn. When they moved to Los Angeles sometime in the 1950's, she never forgave them; I never really knew why. She had a soft spot for the Chicago Cubs, though; probably because they always seemed to be the underdog, and Mother admired a team that never gave up. Then she'd catch herself right in the middle of goofing off and get back to the task at hand, which was, of course, trying to secure information that might save us.

Over and over, Mother struggled to find the weather station, some word from somebody about when the storm was going to let up, or that everything was going to be okay. Perhaps she thought President Eisenhower (Texas-born himself and, therefore, linked to us through the miracle of barbecue and DNA) would be speaking directly to us any minute. Surely Ike would want to let us know he was thinking of us and hoping we were safe.

That's not what she got. What she got was the voice of a man named Gamer Ted Armstrong of the Worldwide Church of God broadcasting all the way from Pasadena, California. I guessed he was a preacher of some sort, but he didn't sound like one to me. I expected a minister's voice to be soothing. The minister's voice at our little milquetoast church was. His voice was so soothing, in fact, that many people nodded off during his sermons each week (a nice guy, but not what you'd call inspirational).

Garner Ted's voice wasn't soothing at all though; it was loud and grating. His message? Not what you'd really need to hear when a tornado was about to sling your whole family out into the next county. While it would have been nice to hear that 'God was really right there beside us after all, not to worry' - encouraging stuff like that - what we heard instead was the shrill voice of some guy in California (who wouldn't know the Seay family from a load of hay, let's be realistic) telling everybody that everything was *not* going to be okay. Not only that, but the United States of America was doomed to famine and pestilence and probably bad haircuts if its citizens didn't repent and soon, brother, or it was all downhill from here. Actually, he didn't really say the part about the bad haircuts; I made that up myself. His was sure an unnerving message, though; I remember that about his words. It was the first of many glimpses throughout my young life that I was probably doomed. *Uh-oh.*

Even at a very early age, I was familiar with repenting. We were close friends, actually; repenting and I were tight. I was only nine, but already I had repented more times than I could remember for infractions which didn't seem all that terrible to me, but loomed huge in Mother's mind - massive transgressions, practically unforgivable acts of sloth and sin which grew worse by the minute - smarting off in church, leaving my bike out in the rain, forgetting to close the refrigerator door, losing my Daddy's good conduct medal while playing army - stuff like that. Mr. Garner Ted Armstrong's take on repenting, though, (what I could hear of it amidst howling winds, the snortling of my three brothers, and trash cans banging down the alley) seemed to come with a catch. According to him, repenting to a God who was already supremely P.O.'d at America meant not only saying you're sorry and promising never to do whatever bad thing you did again, it also included sending off for their Bible study course and, oh, while you're at it, enclosing a big fat check made out to the World Wide Church of God. Apparently, money sent directly to the church founded by Garner Ted's dad, Herbert W., was the most secure route to getting your worthless foot inside Heaven's door.

Of course, I knew my family didn't have any big fat checks. Well, I knew we had checks; just not the big fat part that was needed to keep them legal. Besides, the guy sounded like a weasel to me, but I was only nine - what did I know? Certainly, Mother, whom I knew to be very smart, wouldn't fall for it. *Naaaah, not Mother, not in a million years.* But she did.

Eventually, the tornadoes swirled away and back up into the clouds. The weather let up, but Garner Ted and Herbert W. Armstrong never did. Bible Study courses by the box-load began arriving at our house. Mother poured over each one, sitting up late, puffing on her Tareytons, scouring her Bible for passages and scriptures, underlining everything with a red pencil, and silently praying in that desperate way she had - head down, Bible clutched up close to her heart with one hand, thumb and forefinger of the other hand pinching right at the bridge of her nose, sort of like she looked when she had a sinus headache. Believe me, a sinus headache would have been so much easier to deal with.

There is a lot to consider as a child when someone you love suddenly dives headlong into a new religion and is determined to take you down with them, which, of course, she did. While not too young to form opinions, we all were too young to successfully debate them against Mother. Now armed with her tattered Bible and reinforced with reams of Bible study course material, the mother we all adored had suddenly become a formidable foe in the religion department. She could not be swayed, and we, her children, were the primary targets she had chosen to save from heathenism. I thought the job was probably already too big. *Ready or not, Lake o' Fire, here we come.*

Soon, everything we knew to be true about God, religion, salvation, and even our own tame little church were all tossed up into the air and dropped with a loud *thud!* into the big black drawer in Mother's brain marked 'Suspect/Danger'. There they sat, forevermore, right alongside Hollywood, Catholics, Chief Justice Earl Warren and other liberals, fluoridated water, and the elimination of the poll tax.

You know what the worst thing is about fundamentalist Christians? Well, maybe it's not the *very* worst thing about a lot of them (the ones who lie, kill, cheat and steal and continue to think that's okay because they are "good Christian people"). But here's one of the worst thing to me - okay, I'll just go ahead and say it; say what everybody else in the world thinks but won't mention - they won't shut up.

Even if you agree with them, they won't shut up.

Even if your beliefs are exactly the same as theirs, or you say they are just to shut them up, they won't shut up.

If you don't believe the same, they won't shut up.

If you ask them politely (or not so nicely) to shut up, they won't.

They have to keep talking and talking and talking, yammering on and on about their views of God and Jesus and sin and such until everyone wants to run screaming from the room. Even now, I keep imagining Jesus rocking back and forth, hands over his ears, finally screaming, *"Enough! Just hush! Put a sock in it, will ya?"* It doesn't stop them, though; it just cranks them up. The fundamentalists keep yammering on.

Mother was no exception. She yammered. *OhmyGod, did she ever yammer!* At any family gathering, the one phrase we all muttered to each other over and over was *Don't get her started!* But even if we very carefully didn't get her started, that was only moderate success. Mother pounced upon any opportunity to discuss the end of the world and all of us being tossed into the Lake o' Fire, worthless sinners that we were. The discussion, I'm sure you can see, would sure put a damper on things, party-wise. In my memory, it went something like this:

Mama Loyes: "Somebody turn down the fire under the green beans, please."

Mother: "Fire? Speaking of fire, you know, I'm glad you brought that up. This whole country is going to wind up in a lake of fire if we don't repent. Yep, big ol' lake o' fire. We're gonna roast like weenies on a grill, yessir. We'll melt like a marshmallow at a cookout, like butter in a hot skillet, like salt water taffy in a parking lot on an August day, like a box of crayons in the back window of the car, like..."

See? It was endless. Finally, my grandmother, Mama Loyes, said, "Jo, in this house we treat religion and politics like coats and hang them behind the door." Oh, what a joy it would be to say that tactic worked, but it would be a lie. It lasted about a half hour, really, thirty *looooooooong* minutes of pure torture for us all - Mother biting her lip, her jaw clenching and her face turning red. She nearly popped a cork, if you want to know the truth, and it was absolute misery to watch.

As a young girl already programmed to expect the Four Horsemen of the Apocalypse - Famine, Pestilence, Flatulence and Psoriasis, I think - to come galloping down the Dallas-Fort Worth Turnpike announcing the end of the world, I lived life with my sneakers close by and ready to make a run for it. But witnessing my mother almost spontaneously combust was unsettling. The really hard part was determining which was worse - seeing my mother almost have a stroke, or knowing that God and Mother were both tremendously disappointed in me (and, of course, wondering what a quick dunk into the Lake o' Fire would do to my hair).

Following Mother's conversion to this form of radical fundamentalism, almost everything we had considered to be a normal part of our lives up to that point - Christmas, Easter, Halloween, even Sunday school - suddenly became corrupt and evil. I can testify, yes, verily, I say unto you, there is no greater embarrassment for a young child than having your Mother announce to your playmates that most of the holidays we celebrate in this country are pagan and "...of the devil." Mother believed in Jesus, but that he was born in the fall, and that decorating a Christmas tree was originally part of a pagan ritual. She believed Jesus died for our sins and was resurrected, but that Easter eggs and bunny rabbits were pagan. And Halloween? Well, just forget about that one. *It's a Day of the Dead? Are you kidding?*

Kids from our church, classmates of mine in elementary school, began asking me why they never saw any of us on Sundays. How does a child tell her playmates that her Mother has gone off the deep end? It was hard to explain to them that my mother thought they were all going straight to hell and that everything they were being taught in Sunday school was baloney. For me, the thought of it was agony. It became easier to say, "We just don't go anymore," and let them think whatever they wanted, which was probably that the Seay clan was now a bunch of Devil worshippers. Little did they know that we had God and Jesus coming out our ears at the corner of Glenhaven Boulevard and Keats Drive and that "Mother's religion" was getting nuttier by the minute. I could feel our family beginning to unravel like an old rope.

Growing up in a home with an alcoholic father and Bible-thumping Mother is not unique to my family, I know, and we did manage to get through it. And, to be fair to them both, Daddy quit drinking later on and Mother calmed down about religion, somewhat, as she aged. I think maybe she just wore herself out. Still, sometimes when I look back at it, I am astonished that any of my siblings and I are sane.

Even now, so many years later, this is a hard one for me to write about, and for many reasons. I don't want to dishonor my mother or her faith - the goodness of which was part of her. She was an honorable woman who wanted to do the right thing. As much and as fiercely as I loved her, though, one of the sad facts of her life, in my view, was that her religion made her feel worthless and her politics sometimes made her mean. I wish that weren't true, but it was. And yet, that was certainly not all of who she was.

Like the rest of us in this world, my mother was many things: kind, funny, pretty, smart, talented, creative. But her *far-to-the-right-right-right* political and religious leanings kind of threw a cog right in the middle of all the good things she was, often making me gasp at her gullibility. I feel the shame of it, still, as I write now, not only for the fact that her views often made her into what I thought to be a laughingstock, but that I took such delight in Garner Ted Armstrong's fall from grace some years later. I was thrilled; downright gleeful, actually. I couldn't wait to tell Mother and was practically thumbing my nose at her, *nyah-nyah-nyah,* when I did.

Seems the very-much-married Mr. Garner Ted Armstrong had been having an affair for nine or more years with his secretary or somebody from their organization when Herbert W. found out about it and bounced him out of the church like a bad tithing check.

Garner Ted, naturally, said that he'd been "...wrapped in the chains of Satan..." or something like that. Don't they all blame it on Satan? Anyway, he, Garner Ted, vowed to scrape off his troth and shine it up and give it back to his wife. Not having had anybody to smite in a while, I suppose, his Dad, Herbert W. Armstrong, then smote his sinful son as if he were an Internal Revenue agent and, to my knowledge, never forgave the prodigal bastard. Poor Garner Ted.

Of course, the widowed Herbert W. had his own little bout of hypocrisy to deal with when he fell in love with and married his own secretary (gasp, a divorced woman!), which was something he said no woman should ever be lest she be cast head first into the ever-dreaded Lake o' Fire. Suddenly, the rules changed; at least they did for the new Mr. and Mrs. Herbert W. Armstrong. Big surprise, huh? And isn't that the way it always is? People with a little power and a microphone always manage to bend the rules to serve their own purposes. Astonishing, isn't it? Maybe the Lake o' Fire is all done with mirrors and a Zippo lighter.

My mother, divorced and remarried, a good woman who had fretted over this transgression constantly for years and years deserved better. She deserved to feel worthy of God's love, of making it into Heaven. She deserved better than the messages she got from Garner Ted Armstrong and Herbert W. Armstrong. She deserved to be seen as imperfectly perfect just the way she was. Our family deserved to have her feel that way.

Hearing about both of these incidents befalling the House of Armstrong brought me unspeakable joy, I'll admit. I felt pleasure at pointing and saying, "The emperor has no clothes." Indeed, it seemed obvious to me that the emperors had no clothes, no integrity, no honor, and no business preaching to or condemning others over such things. And nobody will ever change my mind about that.

Of course, Mother being Mother, she said what she always said whenever we locked horns over matters of the spirit, "Well, you know, it's a real dilemma." That usually shut me up. There was nothing more to say. It was, after all, a dilemma and how can you fight against a statement like that? As much as I wanted to rumble and get worked up enough to take a swing at somebody over the whole mess, all I could really do was sit down and be quiet, just like she always made me do in church.

Mother has been gone now for many years - and only a couple of days. As my Ethiopian friend, Solomon, says, "A long time ago is only on the calendar, Jody." He is right about that. In my heart, where the pain of her absence still breathes, the loss of someone so dear to me is a wound still fresh, only a couple of days old. As much as I miss her and as much as I hope to see her again when my time here on earth is done, there is something more that I hope for. I hope Mother feels happy now, deserving, and I hope getting into Heaven was way easier than she thought. I hope God looked up from the sports page when He saw her, His reading glasses sliding down to the end of His nose, and He smiled at her. "Oh, Jo," I imagine Him saying to her, "We're all so glad you're back."

I see this all so clearly in my head that it often brings tears to my eyes. Mother tentatively approaches the throne of God. She is still unsure that this is where she deserves to be. Jesus sits to the right of the Father, working a crossword puzzle. He sees Mother, smiles and gives her a little wave, then leans back, thinking. He taps his front teeth with a pencil. His long legs are stretched out in front of him. Mother notices that Jesus needs a new pair of sandals and that his toenails could stand trimming. Intent on his puzzle, Jesus says to no one in particular, "I need a two-letter word for saint."

God, without looking up, says, "Easy one. Jo." He grins at Mother and she gasps, placing her hand on her heart. Then He motions for Mother to come and sit by Him. Jesus smiles at her and scoots over on the bench, patting the space between himself and his Dad. God says, "We used to have only chairs here on this throne, but I found I often wanted to speak to some of the souls who've just landed. Sometimes people arrive in a group. A bench seemed more practical."

Mother hears a noise, *ta-kink, ta-kink, ta-kink, ta-kink, to-kink ta-kink,* and peers past God to see what the source of the sound is. God motions with His head toward two men locked in a fierce Ping-Pong battle. The Asian guy with the big belly is really sweating - smiling, but sweating. "Buddha and Mohammed," God says. "They go at it like this all the time - wears me out." God notices that Mother looks confused. "Don't let all this bother you, Jo," He says, "It's just one mountain with many roads. See? Over there?" He points to what looks like an elephant in bright orange silk pants playing a game of chess all by himself. "That's Ganesh," God continues, "the remover of obstacles in the Hindu religion. He's a loner, really. Says he has a bad back from all that lifting but I just think he prefers his own company, and that's okay. You'll see them all up here eventually, all the enlightened beings I've sent to earth throughout time to bring all of you back to me."

"People can't seem to figure out how to love each other without some sort of religion involved," God tells her, "and I've always found that a little irritating, if the truth be told. So, I keep sending being after being to show everybody how it's done. Of course, the problem with that method is always that people wind up worshipping the beings I send rather than emulating them. People create one religion after another, thinking one is better than the other. Then, well, then - if you'll excuse the expression - all hell breaks loose, and they wind up killing each other in My name. And that," God says, twisting His head like He's got a kink in His neck, "gets really irritating. But, like I said, it's just one mountain with many roads. Remember that, okay? It may be the most profound thing I've ever said." God suddenly whirls around and shouts out: "ONE MOUNTAIN WITH MANY ROADS." His voice booms and ricochets from cloud to cloud. Mother notices it sounds a lot like John Huston's. God giggles and does a little shuffle. "Man, oh, man," He says, "I just never get tired of doing that." God then smiles sweetly at Mother. She notices He has a space between His front teeth. *Well,* Mother thinks, *after all, nobody is perfect. Funny to get such a sweet smile from God,* she also thinks, *when all I really expected was wrath. Wow. This is so far from wrath it feels like a dream.* She suppresses the urge to laugh out loud.

God places His hand on Mother's shoulder and her whole being is suddenly illuminated by the Light. His eyes are filled with love and compassion for her. "I think I may have failed you, Jo," He says. "I always wanted you to feel how much you were loved by all of us here. I think you worried too much. You were too hard on yourself, and I'm sorry I wasn't as comforting as I should have been. I should have been more apparent, more visible to you, should have let you actually hear and see Me now and then rather than a bunch of preachers who use My name to make a buck. I think that would have helped things go easier for you. Well, We all make mistakes and that was Mine. Can you forgive Me?"

Mother is momentarily dumbfounded, speechless. Her jaw drops. *This is all backwards,* she thinks. *I'm supposed to be the one asking for forgiveness. I never thought it would be like this.* God continues to look into her eyes, waiting for her answer. His hand on her shoulder feels powerful and light at the same time. "Oh, gosh," she says, finally, "Sure."

God smiles at my mother. "Thank you," He says. "Isn't it a great feeling to be forgiven? There's just no better feeling in the world. That's what I keep wanting everyone to experience and not just after they've left the earth. I want them to know it now, *right now.* I've always said it's impossible to know that you are loved without first knowing that you are forgiven. That's what my boy there was all about." God points to His son with His thumb. Jesus looks over at Mother, wiggles his eyebrows up and down, and gives her a little salute, shaking his head 'yes'.

"Regardless of all that," God continues, "I need to give you My official welcome, okay?" Mother nods, suddenly feeling, for the first time in her life, that she and her Creator are close personal friends. She realizes this is how it always should feel. God then leans in by Mother's ear, conspiratorially, and whispers, "Now, this is a little too formal for my tastes, but Peter gets his robes in a twist when We don't do things by the book, even though I tell him it's *My* book." Mother nods again, letting God know she's familiar with people like that. God takes a deep breath and looks again into my mother's hazel eyes. "You made Me proud with your life, Jo, My good and faithful servant," He says. "Welcome home."

Then, because He knows her, God nudges my mother gently in the ribs with His elbow and points to the sports section of the newspaper. "Hey," He says to her, "Four to two in the bottom of the ninth, huh? How 'bout those Cubs?"

"When I stand before God at the end of my life, I would hope not to have a single bit of talent left and could say: 'I used up everything you gave me.'" - Erma Bombeck

"I've told my children that, when I die, to release
balloons in the sky to celebrate that I graduated.
For me, death is a graduation."
- Elisabeth Kubler-Ross

Chapter 27 – Sharing the Lantern

My mother died last night, one month and two days after she entered the Cardiac Care Unit of Methodist Hospital in Dallas. Each day when I saw her, I would ask the question, and each day the answer would be the same. She would fight. But not last night. When I asked the question last night, she was ready to go. And, knowing Mother as I do, I don't even think she threw in the towel. Sure, she was tired and very, very sick, but I don't think it was that at all. I think she finally got to that place past the fear of what's on the other side.

The feeling in the room was so calm it surprised me and my own reaction to her answer surprised me more. Pointing to the respirator, which had sustained her for the past month, she mouthed the word '*off.*'

I said, "You want the machine turned off?"

'*Yes.*'

"You don't want to fight anymore?"

'*No.*'

"Oh, Mother," I said, "that would be such a struggle of a death, but here's what we can do. Your blood pressure is dropping and if you want me to, I'll ask them not to give you the medication to bring it back up. If that's what you want, that's what we'll do."

She nodded '*Yes.*'

"Here's what will happen," I said. "Your blood pressure will continue to drop and your heart rate will slow down. You'll get sleepy, then you'll go to sleep, and then your heart will stop. It won't be painful, and it won't be scary, and it won't be hard. And I'll be right here with you."

My brothers and my sister were there to say good-bye, letting Mother know how much they loved her, that they would miss her, and that we would all be fine. When they went outside to wait, I stayed with her. She was alert and responsive and I was able to make her smile and chuckle. I told her all the things about her that always made me so proud - even little things we never think to mention: how pretty she was; that she could smack a baseball so far; how lovely her hands were, smelling always of salad and Jergen's hand lotion; that she raised us to be patriotic and to believe in God; that she had a temper and a strong sense of integrity; that she cared about things that mattered; and how proud I've always been that my name is Jo, like hers.

I reminded Mother of funny stories about Daddy, Mama Loyes, Daddy Bob and all the relatives, and I told her how I envied her in a lot of ways in being able to be with them so soon. And then I forgave her - for all the times I thought she was a jerk and didn't understand me, and didn't do what I thought she should, or made me do things I didn't want to. And I asked her to forgive me - for all the times I was a jackass and didn't take time for her, or talked back, or didn't tell her the truth, or stomped around and slammed my door, or behaved irresponsibly.

She smiled at me, squeezed my hand and nodded yes.

I said, "Oh, thank you, Mother. You know how easily I do guilt."

She looked at me and shook her head, mouthing the word, *'Don't'*.

I promised her that I would look after everything and make sure that all the little kids, her grandchildren, would never forget Mawmaw. As her blood pressure continued to drop, I knelt beside her bed and prayed, and then I sang a song to her called '*The Eyes of the Lord'*. She held my hand and I could see her drifting back and forth, letting go, crossing the line and then coming back. Just testing the water with a toe, not quite sure. Leaning in close to her, I whispered, "Mother, imagine all the love you've ever felt and all the love you know we feel for you. And then imagine that love like arms all linked together, building a bridge from here to there. And I'll just pick you up and carry you across and hand you to God. It's not hard, Mom, it's not hard."

Finding her Bibles close by, I flipped them both open. Then I read the 23rd Psalm to her, once from the King James Version and once from the Living Bible. As I finished, she shut her eyes and then they opened back up about halfway. I looked at her eyes and the light was gone. At that instant, I saw blood come up in the trachea, and some blood came up in her mouth, and I just took a wash cloth and dabbed it away, then knelt back down beside her bed and held her hand. Lenore, my favorite nurse there, walked in and stood behind me, watching the monitor, her hand resting lightly on my upper back, a gesture of compassion I will remember for all my days. After about a minute, she squeezed my shoulder and said, "It's stopped." I checked my watch, stood, kissed Mother's hand, then leaned over and kissed her forehead. Putting my hand on her head, I said, "Go to the light, pretty girl." And that's what she did. So, that's how my mother died. I feel very proud she got to make the choice about whether to stay or go and we respected that choice, no matter what. I am grateful to so many people, family and friends alike, who supported her and loved her, not just through this final ordeal, but through her life, as well. Believe me when I say she knew it and she felt it, and, with Mother's steel-trap memory, you can bet she'll never forget it.

Nor will I.

My mother was the strongest person I ever met, and, oh - how I adored it when we made each other laugh. She loved her family and friends with lion-like fierceness and loyalty. I am honored and delighted to have known her and to have participated in her life and I feel very, very blessed to have participated in her death.

In 1986 I wrote those words, my gift to my mother and a purge for myself as I sat at my typewriter, remembering my Mom, the night after she died. At times as I was writing, reliving the experience, the pain would become almost unbearable and I would rock back and forth in my chair, hands over my heart, stifling an ache too deep for tears.

Low, animal-like sounds would escape from me, desperately mournful, haunting. I would hear that sound and not know what it was. Now I do. It was the sound of a child with no mother. As I finished writing, the pain came again. I leaned forward, dropping my head. And then I felt it - a hug - arms around both my shoulders from the back, holding me, comforting me in that special way you know is from your Mom, your grandmother, your favorite aunt. As I told my family about it the next night at the funeral home, my sister-in-law gasped. "You felt that, too? My God, I felt that last night," she said. So there it was. The sign. Mother had promised.

Different ideas about spirituality and life after death had taken my mother and me down separate paths. I believe in reincarnation as a means of learning and growing spiritually. Mother was a fundamentalist Christian believing that after death there was a deep sleep while awaiting resurrection. Until we were blue in the face does not nearly describe the depths to which we argued the various points of religion and spirituality over the years, going to the spiritual mat for each other's wayward soul. It always seemed so pointless. And hopeless. But sometimes, you know, just sometimes, I would see a parallel, almost like a picture in my head, of Mother and I on a country road, she walking in one wagon rut and I in the other, sharing the lantern. If oneness with God is the destination, can the avenue we choose matter so much?

That April night we finally tossed down our swords. I said, "Mom, you know, if what you believe is true and you're in a state of unconsciousness, then wake up and we're all together, well, it doesn't really matter because you've been asleep. And, if what I believe is true and it's sort of like going through a revolving door, well, that doesn't really matter, either, because the end result is the same. We're still all together either way. So, the truth here, Mother, is that we really don't disagree about what happens. Our disagreement is about how long it takes. But, if I'm right, give me a sign; let me know, because you know how I love to be right." She grinned at me, nodding yes, rolling her eyes at my silliness.

Mother loved redbirds and they knew it, so her home was also theirs. Territorial creatures, they sang from her trees, preened on her fence, pooped on her car. The night she died, I knelt beside her bed, holding her hand, snuggled in a bubble of underwater light with my Mom. I said, "Every time I see a redbird, I'll think of you." She squeezed my hand, remembering, glad that I did, too. For months and months afterward, redbirds were all I saw. They seemed to be everywhere, so flashy and bright, swirling and soaring and singing gently tapping my memory of her. I'm glad I didn't shoot my mouth off and say, "Every time I see a boa constrictor, I'll think of you." Or a skunk. Or a rat. Life could have gotten complicated.

The first autumn after I moved from Dallas to Portland, I stared out the window at the leaves; brilliant splashes of red and gold, clinging to the limbs against the Oregon rain. Blazing, even as the wind whipped them around. Beautiful, even as Death whispered, *Come with me...* I moved closer to the window - *was I crazy?* The leaves seemed to get more vibrant, their colors more vivid, just before they left the tree. I thought of Mother and how pretty she looked two days before she left when Death came to visit.

A social call, I think it was, a reminder, a promise that the trip would be easy, the path a short one. I was shocked and in awe to see her looking so beautiful and peaceful - smug, even, like she knew a secret just too good to tell. I held her face in my hands, felt Cherokee cheekbones and deep dimples under my palms, saw clear hazel eyes and dark brown hair. *What? Was her hair dark brown again? Was I crazy?* For a moment, I remembered - this is how she looked when I was in grade school 30 years ago! How lovely she was. How proud we were to be Jo's kids, kids who had the prettiest Mom on the block.

A million memories flooded my mind in that instant as I recalled every bruised knee kissed, every fear calmed, every hurt feeling soothed. I remembered our sleepy, pajama-clad parades to the back yard, staggering outside to lie on quilts and watch the stars because Mother got enamored of the Milky Way...being five years old riding in front on horseback with my Mom and hearing her whisper in my ear, "Let's run. Hold on." And feeling her strong arm around my skinny little chest. I saw her bundling us up in quilts on our front porch to watch a Texas thunderstorm, her sure-fire method for confronting any fears of thunder and lightning. So I held her face and recalled each moment and smiled at her. I said, "Remember when you wrapped us in quilts and we sat on the porch and watched the storms?" Mother nodded, perplexed. "Well, it worked," I said, "None of us has ever been afraid of storms. But I bet you didn't know we were all teenagers before we got over our fear of quilts." She grinned. She laughed. She coughed and then touched my head. The thing I loved doing most in the world, I got to do again. I made my Mom laugh one more time. But then it was too much and I started to cry. She reached out through the railing on the bed and touched my face, tapping my chin with her thumb. *Keep your chin up, Jody, it 's only a storm.*

Grief is a sneaky character, a commando, ambushing my heart late at night, battering unresolved sadness from the trapdoors of my soul. Sometimes I think I've never grieved at all - *because i f I had, how could there be this much left?* Other times, I wonder if I'll ever be through. When I am afraid, which is often, it is harder for me to let her go. I am an emotional pygmy, I fear, still five years old and needing my Mom to make everything okay. I wouldn't wish her back here in such poor health; it was a boring, torturous existence for her. But if I could just call her again in the afternoon, wake her up from a nap, and make her laugh one more time, my life would feel so much easier, so much nicer, on this bumpy, grieving path.

So, who was the winner in this game of *Spiritual Jeopardy* my mother and I played for years? Perhaps both of us. Maybe neither of us, and I don't really care at all. I know what I felt and saw, and I know I will always remain humbled by the wonder of it, honored and blessed by the presence of it. And, thank God, that is all that really matters to me anymore.

I have read in more than one place about the light glowing more intensely in people's eyes just before they die, like a candle flickering brightest just before the flame goes out. For some time, I regretted not having seen that with my mother. I've come to realize, though, through time and distance and healing, that what I saw was not only enough but also much more. I got to see her young and beautiful and vibrant, the way she always looks when I shut my eyes and remember her. For this I am so grateful, and because of this, I think I get to see her even more.

I see Mother healthy, vibrant, and smiling at the redbirds. I see her grinning in the Texas sun, laughing at my dumb jokes. But sometimes, you know, just sometimes, I see her walking down that country road, Glory-bound, and I smile as I feel the warmth and bask in the glow from the lantern that we still share.

Mother

"Patriotism is when love of your own people
comes first; nationalism when hate for people
other than your own comes first."
- Charles deGaulle

Chapter 28 – Salute

I am a baby boomer, just as surely a by-product of the urgency of World War II as M&M's, the atom bomb, and the post-war housing where I grew up. One of the things Mother demanded of us was that we be patriotic and love our country and we were happy to comply. A large part of my childhood was spent playing army with my brothers, destroying all the imaginary enemies of America with imaginary bullets. We always won. Our cause was just, our mission true. We were, after all, Americans. The good guys.

My Mother, off the scale to the right in her politics, taught us to love our country, to honor its flag and do the right thing. She also tried to teach us to vote exclusively for conservative Republicans, but that didn't always work out. And that is as it should be.

We are, after all, Americans, diversified yet together when it counts. I grew up loving my Mother, loving my country, standing at attention with my hand over my heart to honor my nation's flag. My heroes were cowboys and colonels. But you know what she couldn't teach me? She could never teach me how *not* to cry when I see our nation's flag or hear the national anthem. Needless to say, I'm an absolute wreck during the Olympics. It's just that something happens inside me when I see Old Glory. My cheeks get hot and I feel that familiar catch in my throat.

There are images in my mind, reservoirs of memories, of friendship, of patriotism, and of unity, that I will always remember. When I am very old and can't recall the day of the week or even the year I was born, I will remember these. August 19, 1958, Forestburg,

Texas: my sister was born yesterday. I am eight years old, almost nine, shuffled off to spend the week with Aunt Roxie and Uncle Meb. They run the Post Office in this tiny town. Each day I watch Uncle Meb raise the American flag out front and I stand at attention, hand over my heart, being as American as I can be, proud of something I barely understand.

Each evening Uncle Meb lowers the flag and folds it into a perfect triangle. "Why do you fold it up like that?" I ask, and Uncle Meb, a World War I vet and Texas Democrat, stares at me as if he is astonished we are related.

"Because that's the way it's done," he says.

This morning he hooks the flag to the rope and hands both to me. "You raise the flag today," he says, "for your sister, our newest American." I am thrilled, I am honored, I am terrified. I pull on the rope slowly, clutching the end of the flag, *I can't let the flag touch the ground, Dean says so. If it touches the ground you have to burn it and I bet they don't have another one around here anywhere - gotta keep the rope straight, don't get it tangled, that would really be stupid.* I glance at Uncle Meb. He holds his white straw cowboy hat over his heart, and I see the blue-green tattoo on his forearm. I don't know what it says or what it is, only that he got it when he was a soldier and still had hair. Today, his bald head glistens in the sunlight, and there's a crease in his forehead from his hat.

The hook on the rope makes a metallic *clang* against the pole and I look up in time to see the flag snap like a towel and billow out in the hot August wind. *Yes,* I think, *my sister is an American. Like me.*

October, 1968, Austin, Texas: America is neck-deep in Vietnam; young men I know have already died there. Nobody I know except my Mother trusts the government to tell the truth. I struggle with my feelings about the war constantly. Bobby Kennedy was killed in June. I love my country. My brother is a Marine. I don't want anybody else to die.

I am walking with a crowd of people into the University of Texas stadium for a football game. The Longhorn band booms out the national anthem, and we all stop and sing the words. The day is bright and still and the American flag just hangs there like a week-old dishrag. *This is us*, I am thinking, *this is how we feel, like we've lost our national snap.* My heart feels heavy, but I keep singing, and as we get to the final phrase, *Oh, say, does that star spangled banner yet wa-aaaaave...some* guy behind me says, "Aw, come on, flag," and the breeze picks up and the flag unfurls and blows wildly, like our hair, in the autumn wind. I am crying and thinking: *All these people are Americans. Like me. Oh, please, God, let it feel good to be us again.*

July 4, 1982, New Orleans, Louisiana: I am visiting my friend Don, a handsome, sweet, sensitive and funny man who dances with the New Orleans Ballet Company. We are unlikely pals, except that we love each other and make each other laugh really hard. Don is from Long Island, New York and is absolutely crazy in love with New Orleans. We are walking through the French Quarter down to the Mississippi River to watch the fireworks. Don is telling me all the things he loves about this place - the history, the diversity, the fun-loving spirit of the people, the tradition. I am telling him that the whole place seems nuts to me, that all anyone cares about is partying and that it feels like being on the Midway at the Texas State Fair, only hard-core. "Don't these people care about anything that matters?" I say to him.

"Of course, they do, Jody," Don replies. "They're Americans, too." When we get to the river, there are thousands of people, it seems like; so many of them we can't get anywhere near the shore, so we stand in the street up the hill. Gigantic fireworks boom and sizzle and whine across the night sky, and all the people yell when a good one goes off and wave their arms in the air and slosh beer all over each other. The evening is hot and humidity hangs in the air like a wet diaper. I feel my shirt sticking to my back.

Suddenly, I hear it, a sound almost like a choir, rumbling, rolling up the hill from the river like a wave. It is the voice of ten thousand drunk, happy Yanks singing God Bless America on the

Fourth of July. I am instantly ashamed that I judged them, that I thought they didn't care. I am crying and laughing; Don is crying and laughing. And we lean on each other in the middle of a street in New Orleans that smells of beer and pee and the sweat of ten thousand other Americans just like us. Don grabs me in a headlock and scruffs my hair. "See, silly?" he says.

September, 1985, Dallas, Texas: my nephew, Johnny, is in kindergarten and calls me to recite The Pledge of Allegiance and sing God Bless America over the phone. He is shocked that I know the words to both and is excited when I pledge and sing right along with him. He doesn't believe me when I tell him I learned them both in school like he did. He doesn't believe I was ever in school. He thinks I have always been this age, this size, this gray, and that my purpose on the planet is to tell him to stand up straight and say please and thank-you. I explain to him the importance of saying, "...and to the *Republic, for which it stands...*" rather than, "...and to the *Republicans, for which it stands...*" And then, just for the heck of it, we sing The Eyes of Texas.

January 27, 1991, Portland, Oregon: America is at war and I am angry that my patriotism is questioned because I don't want Americans to die. My personal vow, though, my secret oath is that I will never let American soldiers feel like they did after Vietnam - dishonored by their nation and deserted by their government. It is Super Bowl Sunday and I turn on the TV to watch the game. What I see is Whitney Houston, with a voice like God's own special angel, singing the National Anthem. She doesn't dink around with the melody; she doesn't forget the words. She sings strong and pure and the music floats up and out of her and swirls around in the heavens. Through my tears I see thousands of people in the stadium waving teeny American flags, and in a flash, in the core of me, I get it. They have made the same personal vow; their secret oath is the same as mine. And, war or no war, suddenly it feels good to be us again.

September 11, 2001: we have suffered a major blow. Big chunks of our nation have just been exploded with jet airliners. Thousands of people have died, including police officers and fire fighters and rescue workers. All of us around the world have watched our television sets, horrified, wondering how this could have happened and, more importantly - *why?* One of the news anchors is talking about a telegram from somebody in Pakistan that read, simply: "Today, we are all Americans." I stare at the television, crying, as I hear Peter Jennings talk about this. The scene shifts, and we watch firefighters unfurl a huge American flag from the top of one of the buildings still upright amidst the smoke and rubble. My throat closes up.

Bloodied, battered, scraped up, but we are Americans, still standing. Americans. The world, we are still standing. We are all in this together, I am thinking, *Oh please, dear God, let it be so.*

"Without forgiveness, there's no future."
- Desmond Tutu

Chapter 29 – The Hero

In the end, as he lay dying, I went to see him. I flew back to what I used to call "home" to see the brother I'd not spoken to in years. I was angry at him for using up women the way he did, for wasting his life. I was afraid of being duped by the con man he'd become. Now gone from there for so long, being back brought memories of the blisters of shame burned on all our souls by a raging father. My blisters burst and healed; my brother's never did. The life he created from that raw and jagged wound was one long, endless series of bad choices, choices which gobbled everyone in our family up at one time or another. We were shredded by it, unraveling over time like a rotting burlap sack. Now my brother's lungs and heart, only thirteen months older than my own, were shutting down, snuffing the life out of the most fragile of us.

The only light was from the TV. The room was choked with cigarette smoke and the smell of bachelor men. My brother was sitting up in bed taking long drags off a Marlboro, as if the nicotine and the smoke itself were his Life Force, the only things filling him up, the only things reminding him he was still alive. His pack of smokes and Zippo lighter were oddly mingled on the nightstand with his medications, his bronchial dilator, and the coiled tube to his oxygen tank, which was turned off and standing by the bedroom door like a sentry.

My brother's hair, thick and wavy like mine, had never grayed, unlike mine, and now lay flat and dull against his head. Slashed across his face, almost as vivid as a scar, was the look of a man - a boy, really - who had been trying to die in one way or another for most of his life. His surprise in seeing me triggered a coughing spasm lasting only seconds but seeming like forever. Lungs, wet and tattered, rattled and slapped against his chest wall, and there was a sound like denim ripping from somewhere deep inside him. For a big man he looked skeletal - fragile, just as I'd always known.

"You make a wrong turn?" he asked, finally, stubbing out his smoke, milking the words from his throat as he pulled on his oxygen mask. I rolled the canister over beside his bed and twisted the knob until I heard the *sssssssss* of life-giving air. A gray, noxious haze stayed suspended in the room, floating in front of the TV screen like a cloud of doom.

"I came to see you," I said, feeling awkward, off-balance, vulnerable. "Heard you were sick." I fumbled for more to say to him, for whatever he needed to hear to go on. My heart, hardened and guarded against him for so long, began to split open in my chest. My hands trembled. Words and sorrow and tears and regret formed a bulging, soggy lump in my throat. Beyond all the dysfunction in my family; beyond all the crap he pulled; beyond our collective anger at him for it, this was what I knew: My big brother was dying, the first of the five of us to go. This was the jumping-off place. I had to make it okay for him to leave and I had to do it for both of us.

"Yeah, well, it shouldn't be long now, that's what they tell me." He lifted the mask and wheezed the words out, like a bagpiper squeezing for each sound, then pushed himself up on skinny arms. His Vietnam-era Marine Corps tattoo flexed into a mashed, bluish-green mess on his wasted upper arm and his bones shook from the weakness, from the closeness of death. I helped him lean forward to try to clear his lungs, to stave off that feeling of drowning. Jamming another pillow behind his back, I was shocked at how his body had gone away. Then it was too much. The pain of it struck me like a snakebite, as piercing as an ice pick in my gut. I slid to my knees beside his bed and sobbed into my hands - for his wasted life, for the distance between us, for whatever it was that blew us all apart.

I wanted to tell him *Thank you for grabbing the reins the day my horse bolted and ran off with me; thank you for saving one of the twins from drowning at Turner Falls; thank you for pulling Don to shore when his legs cramped at the lake. Thank you for being the hero I never forgot.* But I was crying too hard to get it all out so I just rested my face on the smelly sheet and looked at him. "I want you to know," I whispered, "that I knew the you who lived inside before Daddy convinced you that you were so bad. It's not true, what he said, and it never was." Through the smoke, my brother coughed and touched my hair.

BUT THIS ISN'T THE TRUTH.

This is a story. Even though I'd seen it so many times in my head it felt real, still it wasn't. This was my *fantasy* about how my final good-bye to my brother would happen.

Many years ago, I read a magazine article by Andrew Vachss, a writer and attorney who often represents abused children. The focus of this article was emotional abuse and how the scars from that are often worse and longer lasting than those from physical abuse. I cut the article out and mailed it to Dean. I enclosed a letter to him about our childhood from my point of view, about the hard parts, which were in all honesty, really hard. Oddly stitched into the quilt of an upbringing often full of laughter and fun, there was also alcoholism and rage, and rage trumps fun almost every time. At the bottom of the letter I wrote: *I want you to know that I knew the You who lived inside before Daddy convinced you that you were so bad. It's not true what he said - and it never was.*

I didn't hear back from my brother and didn't expect to, really. I just needed him to know that I saw him. His lungs were so bad for so long, then his gall bladder exploded and then his pancreas went haywire, then peritonitis nearly did him in. His body was a mess - banged up, diseased, worn out. Even though I figured he'd be the first of the five of us to go, still, I was always surprised he had managed to live as long as he did.

I was in Tulsa on business when I got the call from my sister Peggy that Dean was dying. Peggy, with the cow-catcher of truth attached to the front of her, pushed me, just like she'd done all her life, into seeing what was real, into telling the truth, and doing what was right. I needed to forgive our brother so he could go on to the next life, and I needed to forgive him so that I could live with myself in this one. I remembered the night Mother died and how, besides "I love you," the most important thing we said to each other was "I forgive you." It didn't matter what for - it was for everything, for anything. I will be eternally grateful to my kid sister for leaning on me.

I picked up the phone and dialed Dean's number. It was late. As I was dialing, a wave of compassion flooded over me. It felt like a warm, golden light; peaceful, from a place of silence. It felt almost like a secret, a treasure entrusted to my care. Dean's wife, Laura, answered the phone then held it to his ear. Dean was on oxygen and lots of morphine and couldn't speak at that point, but opened his eyes when he heard my voice, Laura told me later.

"Dean," I said, "this is important and I need you to know this before you go. I love you. I forgive you and I want you to forgive me. I'll be in Dallas tomorrow morning at ten. Mike will pick me up at the airport and we'll come straight over, so I'll see you then. But if it's too hard, Dean, listen, don't wait on me, don't stay one more second than you have to. You just go ahead and go on; it'll be like diving off Turner Falls. Dean, listen to me. This is important. Don't worry. And don't be afraid. You will be fine. Don't worry. Just go be with Mother." My big brother died the next morning at 5:30, January 17, 2005. He was fifty-six years old.

And that's the truth.

"All same people, God say." - Quanah Parker

Chapter 30 – Courage

Bravery shows up in a life in many forms, some of them are often a surprise. While, for most of my years, I ached to be heroic, there was part of me just weak-kneed at the thought of danger, even though I'd fight to the death to protect my mother or my siblings. Of that much I was sure. The part of me which took to heart all my mother's predictions of doom lurking about just waiting to snatch her children away from her terrified me, too.

I couldn't stand the thought that I was secretly Zeke, the Cowardly Lion; Bert Lahr, cleverly disguised as a young girl from Texas named Jody. It was this fear of fear which drove me to take every dare tossed my way, to keep up with brothers and cousins and neighborhood rowdies and whoever else decided to do something dangerous and thrilling just to see if we could all live to tell about it.

Good stories were what my boisterous family thrived on, so to be able to tell one about some near-death experience, well, that just made it all the better, especially if something funny happened right in the middle of it.

For example, my cousin Herbie decided once, a long time ago, that we could get some really incredible photographs of car lights streaking by if we set up a camera and tripod on the median of Stemmons Freeway in Dallas and then left the shutter open as the cars whizzed by. This would involve, of course, the two of us sprinting, *at night*, out to the middle of the four-lanes-on-each-side freeway and back, hauling a tangle of photography equipment as cars raced past us at seventy miles per hour or more (probably way more). Dangerous? Sure, but not so much more dangerous than other some of the other dangerous things we'd done. Besides, we reasoned, we were sober, so how badly could we screw it up?

Well, we gathered all the stuff we needed, drove to the perfect spot and parked his Mother's '64 Dodge on the shoulder. As we stood there with the cars and trucks barreling past, cameras and gear slung over our necks, the wind blasted our hair wildly around our heads. My stomach began jumping; doing some weird little tap dance in my gut and my heart was pounding so hard I could see it beat through my shirt. There was no blood in the lower half of my body, I knew it. All of my blood was in my throat, but *no way* was I going to let my cousin know I was scared out of my mind.

Herbie spotted an opening in the traffic and shouted, "Now! Go!" We took off running and, as soon as we did, I got charley horses in both my thighs, cramps that nearly brought me to my knees. I was paralyzed; my legs just wouldn't move. The pain ripped through me. It was intense, ragged and excruciating. I screamed and shouted out something that was a cross between a screech and a yodel - like a big truck hitting its air brakes while crashing into an Oktoberfest celebration. I think that's most likely how it sounded. *I am screwed, I know it.* Luckily, the noise that honked out of me was loud enough that my cousin looked back to where I was, stranded in the second lane of Stemmons freeway with cars and trucks bearing down on me. Then, never missing a step, like a battlefield hero, Herbie circled back, grabbed all my gear and looped it around his neck. Even though we were much closer to the Dodge than the median, my cousin slung my arm over his shoulder and dragged me out to the middle of the freeway, scraping the toes of my sneakers along the concrete as if I were a wounded comrade-in-arms he was about to load onto a chopper. *After all, we couldn't miss such a terrific shot, could we?*

Now, the streaking car light photo would have been a good story on its own, but the fact that my leg cramps nearly got us killed and we still got the shot, well, that made it a great story. See what I mean?

A delightful man I knew in Tulsa, Oklahoma, Gil Baker, (now deceased) was talking about his experience in World War II as a nineteen year old Second Lieutenant Bombardier in the Army Air Corps. "Yep," he said, "all us young bucks raced out as soon as we heard about Pearl Harbor to sign up and go fight this war to prove to each other we weren't the chickenshit bastards we knew in our hearts we were."

And I thought, *Is this really the reason we fight most wars? Is this what the people who think up the wars are counting on, that fear of having others think we're afraid?* I can relate to all of it, truthfully, but it was so refreshing to hear someone from that generation finally voice it.

I found out I was brave, though, the night my mother died. Death is scary and messy and smelly. It's not something many of us want to stick around for. And yet, there is something almost elegant about it, something certainly spiritual and almost joyful, in a way, like being witness to a birth.

There are so many emotions surrounding it all, especially when it's someone you love so dearly, as I did Mother. Part of me, the little kid part who could not bear the thought of being on this earth without her, wanted to pull my shirt up over my head and run screaming from the room. The bigger part, though, the brave part, kept thinking *This is the last thing I can do for her.* And so I stayed and helped my Mom get born into Heaven. That's what death is, of course; to me it is. Death is simply a birth into the next life.

Since the night my mother died, I've helped three other of my dearest friends pass on as well. And I'm so, so glad I did. When I talk about it to people and tell them the truth about all the aspects of it, I also tell them that if they stay in the room and help the person they love cross over, it will change their own life forever. Forever. And it does, if only they are brave enough to stay in the room.

Sometimes, some of those lucky times life hands us, I know we can coast into courage on the power of somebody else's thoughts about us. (I don't know about you, but this feels like a big, fat miracle to me - a Godplop!) When someone we admire sees us as braver than we feel we are inside, where it counts, well, sometimes, through the grace of

God, we can become that. And I know that's true because it happened to me way back in 1978 when I met Janie French.

Janie was an amazing woman who, along with Annie Duggan, developed and taught a particular type of movement work all over the world. It's called DFA, or the Duggan-French Approach. I find I rather enjoy knowing people who are world-famous.

One of the wonderful parts about Janie was that she connected with everyone because she could see that kernel of goodness and power that lives in each of us - even me. That was the good part. The tougher part was that Janie was perfectly willing to kick my ass whenever she thought I wasn't being the best Jody I could be, the one she saw all the time. By the time Janie died in 2001, I was well on my way to being as brave as she saw me - even without the threat of having my ass kicked. Oh, I miss her. In my novel, <u>The Second Coming of Curly Red</u>, Cory Miller (one of the lead characters) has her life changed when she realizes the hero, Jimmy Heron, sees her as brave, which is not how she sees herself at all. She suddenly goes from "spineless" to finding pieces of her vertebrae. 'Suddenly' is the operative word, I think, because change and realization of personal power can happen so quickly it'll take your breath away. I am including the following paragraph from that story here, not only because I think it is pretty - which I do - but because I think it is significant.

Transformation can take place in an instant, faster than the flicker of a thought. Courage can come out from its hiding place when least expected, when it is needed most. As gently as a whisper through the trees or a shadow across the canyon wall courage pushes its way through, upward past fear and then settles itself across the shoulders like a comfortable old sweater. Things change, shift, making room for the beating of brave heart. And once courage has found its place, there is no going back. Not ever.

What I know is that, for me, there is no going back. Not ever. I will stand tall - all five feet, five inches of me - and speak the truth of my life, even though an "in your face" lesbian is not what I'll ever be.

An "in your heart" lesbian is a much more appealing description of who I want to be - how I want to be - in this world. Chances are my courage will never be tested in any of the ways I thought. I'll never find myself in a foxhole on a battlefield somewhere, unless things here at home between the Republicans and Democrats get really heated up. Then, of course, I guess I'll have to do fifty thousand or so push-ups and go buy a Howitzer or something. I hope not. I really do hope the pen will always still be mightier than the sword, that being able to write my truth will mean more to me than eliminating those who don't agree with it or who don't want to read it.

As I mentioned, a few years ago I penned my first novel, The Second Coming of Curly Red. It was about a seventy year old man who is befriended by a lesbian couple after the tragic death of his wife. It was also about love and courage and compassion and understanding. It was about the inherent danger waiting to take us all over when we don't stand up and speak out for fairness and truth.

In the process of promoting my book, traveling all around the country, what I realized was that the writing of it made me braver than I ever thought I'd be in real life. Certainly, there's nothing like popping out of the closet to a big chunk of the reading public to let you know where you stand in the courage department. I hadn't actually planned it that way.

In books about writing, they always say, "Write about what you know." Well, I certainly know about being a lesbian, but it's not *all* I know. And I can't even say I was completely out of the closet when my novel was published, but that all changed, and quickly.

At a book reading in New York City the sign interpreter brought an elderly deaf man up to me to autograph his copy of my novel. "He wants to tell you something," she said, "in his own voice."

I smiled at him and he reached out and held my face in his hands, then kissed my forehead. "I love you," he said, "you are beautiful. It makes me feel good to see you." Now, I don't know anything about this man's life. All I know is that I wrote a story that touched his heart and he needed to let me hear that from him. Speaking as a writer, it was one of those moments that make you remember why you do it at all. It is a memory that will stick with me, one I am so very proud of and one that will never let go of me.

When I think back on bouncing out of the closet, it was easier than lots of other things I've done in my life. Actually, it all happened so sweetly. I wrote the book. It was a big hit. The book and I just sort of tumbled out of the closet in a heap. And, of course, it's not as if lesbians are groundhogs - see our shadow or get spooked and run right back into the closet. Once you're out, you're pretty much out! So, we (the book and I) toppled out of the closet, landing in the lap of America who scruffed our heads and said, "Silly. So, what's the big deal?"

I have to keep asking that, too, "So, what's the big deal?" I can't speak for every lesbian but, for me, being one is so much more than what people think. It is so much more than just being attracted to other women, so much more than just being good at sports, so much more than only leading when I dance, so much more than being able to sing along in Anne Murray's key. For me, it is like belonging to this wonderfully sweet, exclusive, almost secret club of women who are brilliant, beautiful, funny, kind, talented, dedicated, compassionate, spiritual and real.

At an afternoon cookout in Dallas one summer, we were celebrating someone's birthday. Five or six of the women were playing croquet. Somebody came out in the backyard with a camera and these women, as if on cue, suddenly all turned to the side, posing like majorettes, hands on their hips, one leg cocked in the drill team "parade rest" position, their croquet mallets balanced across their arms as makeshift batons. I thought, *"These are the prettiest, funniest women I know. Why can't the rest of the world see them as I see them?"* It breaks my heart that the rest of the world doesn't really understand them; doesn't know their hearts or what they care about; doesn't know that they love their country and their families as much as anyone else does. And that really is a big deal.

Do I have regrets about any of my life? Sure. I regret never having come clean about my life to Mother before her death. I regret the times I've hidden out or hung back or felt unworthy in this world. I regret the times I've succumbed to the temptation of being as hate-filled as the people who want to kill me. Avoiding that is my biggest spiritual challenge. I regret, most of all, the times I wasn't true to myself, for those are the hardest ones of all to remember. Those memories are in my pack, though, and I will carry them - not until I'm too weak to carry them anymore, but until I am strong enough to put them down. Should be any day now.

Despite what my Mother always worried about, *dead in a ditch is* most likely not where I'll wind up, but I could be wrong. We'll see. Life is tricky sometimes and could quite easily throw me a curve. Until the circumstances of my life's end make themselves apparent, though, this is my truth - my story and I'm stickin' to it, as they say. Because, after all is said and done, beyond all my worries and all my fears, this much I know: I am from Texas. I am my Mother's daughter. And living an authentic life is the bravest thing I'll ever do.

"It takes courage to grow up and become who
you truly are." - e.e. cummings

*"Unless a reviewer has the courage to give
you unqualified praise, I say ignore the
bastard." - John Steinbeck*

About the Author

Jody Seay is an award-winning author as well as the creator, producer and host of the television show, <u>Back Page</u>. She has also been an Advanced Certified Rolfer for over thirty years.

She's originally from Dallas, Texas and is the granddaughter of a cattle rancher. Her writing is a combination of tender, funny, and common sense. It reflects the humor and wisdom of fellow Texan, Molly Ivins, shaken together with the type of tales and yarns spun by American populist, Will Rogers. Jody Seay has always believed in the power of stories to change our world.

In this memoir, <u>Dead in a Ditch</u>, Jody invites the reader to take a look at her 'family story album' as she and her siblings manage to survive all the various ways their mother thought they would die. These snapshots of tales introduce us to a little girl who took every double-dog dare to prove her bravery and re-introduces her as an adult who has realized the meaning of a life well-lived. From this collection we get to experience the wackiness of growing up in a loud and rowdy Texas brood, what it meant to come out as a lesbian in a conservative family, and witness the courage it takes to live an authentic life.

Jody says, "I do see myself as grounded, intelligent, funny, outspoken, and liberal. My writing reflects those characteristics along with a touch of tenderness, which I think touches people's hearts. If I can write a story that makes people laugh and cry, then that makes me a happy girl. Indeed, if I can write a story that breaks my own heart and I still feel good at the end of it, I know I've put another one over the center field wall."

Jody now lives in Oregon with her partner, their yappy dog and a mean cat.

Susan Anderson Nolen

(Jody's cousin Susie - her favorite cousin in New Mexico)

I'm proud of you, Jody

The first edition of *The Seventh Dragon* was called 'the zen of piano tuning.' It wone the Western States Book Award for creative nonfiction and became a minor classic among music lovers.

The second edition (Unlimited Publishing, 2005) draws on Sullivan's 25 years as a piano tuner and on recent scholarship about early piano history. The mystery remains, but it's now richer than before.

Anita T. Sullivan
illustrations by Sarah Bienvenu

Order from:
seventhdragon.com,
Amazon, Barnes & Noble, or
local independent bookstores
1-58832-131-2 (Cloth)
1-58832-130-4 (Paper)

Tulsa Yoga Therapy

Knowledge ~ Guidance ~ Support
Private sessions ~ Group classes ~ Workshops

www.tulsayogatherapy.com
Phone 918-835-5927
Email stephenyogi@yahoo.com

Stephen Saunders LMT
YOGA THERAPIST

Good Luck Jody
Love S

by Caroline Miller

Both books are avaliable at www.amazon.com and
www.barnesandnoble.com
http://www.carolinemillerbooks.com/

"I just want to
read the book."

Best, CONSUELO

JODY'S FAVORITE
SQUEE

says, "Well done!"

Best wishes to
Jody
from
Jim Wygant
www.jimwygant.com

Jim's novels, *Confessions of a Lie Detector*,
The Spy's Demise, and *Jessica's Tune,* are all
available online from Amazon or Barnes
& Noble.

Ivan Braiker
Chief Executive Officer

11241 Slater Avenue NE, Suite 201
Kirkland, WA 98033
www.hipcricket.com

phone 425.202.0833
mobile 206.679.3025
fax 425.827.1561
email ivan@hipcricket.com

hipcricket®

Bunkn' With You in the Afterlife

This ecumenical lesbian cowgirl musical begun originally as an idea out of a book: the people to whom we are connected on the earth plane we will be with in the afterlife. Bunkin' With You in the Afterlife, has traveled quite a dusty trail to end up where it is today. From a thought to a song, to a kernel of an idea, to a full-blown musical comedy being produced by Melinda Pittman and the geniuses at BroadArts Theatre in Portland, Oregon.

Award-winning author, speaker, and TV host, Jody Seay, wrote this musical about love, loss, redemption, and spiritual awakening to satisfy two issues. One, she wanted to confront, in a humorous and respectful way, all of the major religions which feel that they must be at war with each other all the time in order to prove that theirs is the only path, when, as she sees it, there is just one mountain with many roads. Two, she had grown weary of seeing the spiritual lives of gays and lesbians marginalized. Jody has set out to correct the assumption that the spiritual lives of people who have a different sexual orientation somehow don't matter or are "less than."

Featuring several original songs and parody, Bunkin' With You in the Afterlife is a romp. Minnie Rhodes and her Many Roads Ministry, Cowgirls for the Lord is a group of lesbians who ride around on horseback through very conservative southern Oregon spreading the good news – not of having been saved – but, indeed, of never actually having been lost. Along the way, we hear their stories of love, joy, sadness, redemption, forgiveness and, in the end, we watch their hearts open with acceptance – for themselves, each other, and for unconditional love from their Creator.

"To Jody, a bright spirit"

Nicholas French, Ph.D.
Certified Advanced Rolfer
Diplomate Jungian Analyst

Dallas, Texas   214-357-7571

Celebrating Creative Communication
C3 Publications
George B. Wright
Publisher

3495 NW Thurman Street; Portland, Oregon 97210
Phone: 503-223-0268
Website: www.c3publications.com
Email: georgec3pub@comcast.net

Tech Scribe, Inc.

Writing & Editing Services
Technical & Marketing Documentation

Chéla Wallace
cwallace@techscribenow.com

Phone: 503.936.7157
Fax: 503.214.5406
Web: techscribenow.com

---

*"JODY'S FOREVER
FRIEND AND THE
VERY BEST REASON
TO VISIT SANTA FE"*

Sheryl Reese

"Congrats Jody!"

Kathy & Keith

Sunset High School
SunsetAlumniAssociation.com
sunsetbisons@gmail.com

P.O. Box 225276
Dallas, Texas 75222-5276

joe whitney

jd **WHITNEY ENTERPRISES INC.**

1652 Sylvan Ave., Dallas, Texas 75208
(214) **941-8888**   **Fax:** (214) 941-2332
E-Mail: joedwhitney@gmail.com

Evelyn Sharenov

Member: National Book Critics Circle
Visit my website at:
    www.redroom.com/author/evelyn-sharenov

Nonfiction editor: Thumbnail Magazine
    http://thumbnailmagazine.com

Back Page (Television & Internet Show)

So, how was it you got to do a TV show? You
pull a gun on somebody?
- Geneice Gray, Dallas, Texas

Since 2004, when Jody Seay conceived of Back Page, the show has
been featuring writers of all stripes, mostly from the Pacific Northwest,
(although Jody has been known to host authors from as far away as
Toronto, Tulsa, Ft. Worth, and Isis Cove, NC - as long as she felt there
was a good story being told). In 2006, Back Page went from a fairly
amateur show taped in Jody's office with one camera panning back and
forth to a much more sophisticated program with a 3-camera setup,
nice set and great graphics. The show is now produced at Oregon State
University in Corvallis. The programs are streamed out to public,
university, and governmental sites across Oregon, wherever programs
from Oregon Wireless Instructional Network can be seen, as well, as
Southern Oregon Public Television and on the internet.

Back Page is the only television show in Oregon devoted to writing,
authors, and with the focus on the story behind the story. Jody believes
that everybody has a story to tell. Everybody. And when we hear each
other's stories, we connect. By honoring that connection, we have a
chance to change the world; it is very difficult to stay angry at a person
once you realize that you have more in common than not. That belief
makes Back Page a most noble cause; a cause writers believe in and
viewers want to see.

The Back Page Mission Statement says this:

> *It is through the writing and telling of stories that we*
> *share our common humanity. From that one step, we*
> *realize that we are all in this together and more the same*
> *than different. This is the essence of enlightenment; it is*
> *the learning tool, the implement of empathy and*
> *connection, sought throughout human history.*

> *The stated purpose of the educational and informative*
> *TV program, Back Page, is a two-pronged idea. First*
> *connect writers and readers, to spotlight the creative*

*process and motivation, and to uncover the story
behind the story. Second, it is the intent of the
creators to produce a vehicle by which authors,
especially new authors, can promote their work to
a large number of people and not have to bear the
financial burden of that marketing format.*

*Far too many good books and great stories go
unnoticed due to lack of promotional funding. By
bringing these books to the public, everybody wins
– readers, authors, publishers, bookstores as well
as organizations and individuals that help sponsor
this program. Our connection to each other is then
strengthened with each wonderful story told, and
our communities, our nation and our world are all
the better for it.*

Indeed, we are more than words, more than language. We are stories –
each of us, a collection of tales of triumph and joy, sagas of loss and
mourning. We are, individually and collectively, a genetic mish-mash
of family history, of well-turned phrases, stories told and then re-told,
of crackpot ideas, and even occasional piercing brilliance. The soup
pot of stories in which we have all tumbled like chunks of turnips now
bubbles and stews, softening our centers, turning us golden around the
edges, making us vulnerable and oh-so-human, and so very much more
the same than different. This is what we learn from the writing and
telling of stories.

Back Page is a show about the story behind the story. It is a way for
viewers to get to know Oregon writers and to be allowed a peek at the
back page, to find out the motivation for each book written, every story
told. It is a way for us to discover our commonalties and appreciate
them, rather than staring in rage or bewilderment at our differences.

Words matter; we surely must know that by now. They inspire us,
ignite us, open our hearts and make us laugh 'til tears stream down
our cheeks. We are connected by words, mind to mind, heart to heart.
In the end, what we know is that words light our way on this bumpy,
human path and remind us, as our shoulders brush against each other's
in the darkness, that we are all in this together, making our way home.

MASTERPIECE SMILES

BY
JAN L. COBBLE, DDS

Jody says, "If God needed dental work, he'd call this guy. Really."

"Congratulations on your new book. Is this one going to be an award-winner, too?

Cynthia Griffin

Georgie E. Sawyer
"Jody, you are a master storyteller and one funny Texan. Hurry and get this book out so I can read it!"

Who is Cap't Bob? Where is Cap't Bob?
- Reny Frog

'Way to go Jody. We can't wait to see your cowgirl musical (*Bunkin' With You in the Afterlife*) and to read your new book (*Dead in a Ditch*)."

Best wishes, Jody
Hope all will be successful!

Betty Roberts

Author of "*With Grit and By Grace: Breaking Trails in Politics and Law, A Memoir*"

Koho Pono

A multimedia publishing company exploring the evolution of consciousness & pursuit of life's meaning

Welcome to Koho Pono multimedia publishing - a publishing firm specializing in exploring the evolution of consciousness & pursuit of life's meaning. This includes humor, awareness, innovation, process improvement, change management, and strengthening relationships for business and individuals. We support the evolution of consciousness and the pursuit of relevance in life by improving systems and relationships at any level.

We hope you share our interest in fiction (individuation & psychological hero's journeys) as well as non-fiction (business, self-help, & new age titles).

Website: http://kohopono.com/

Email: info@kohopono.com

www.JODYSEAY.com

Heaven's way of ensuring that I would see the humor in most of life's situations was to launch me into the world under unusual circumstances. My mother's water broke with me at the Spike Jones concert at Fair Park in Dallas, Texas on October 25, 1949. I was born breech and dry two days later, an impatient, silent and brooding baby...On the fifth day of my life, a nurse came into my mother's room and said, "Well, she finally cried today." And I've not hushed since. - Jody Seay

More

Jody Seay

Author of Novels, Short Stories, Essays and Snotty Letters

Website: http://jodyseay.com/

CPSIA information can be obtained at www.ICGtesting.com
Printed in the USA
LVOW071549061011

249423LV00002B/158/P